SEASON OF PEACE
Devotional

*100 Inspirational Messages
To Help You Find Peace From
Anxiety, Fear, and Panic Attacks*

RUSSELL POND

SEASON OF PEACE
Devotional

100 Inspirational Messages
To Help You Find Peace
From Anxiety, Fear, and Panic Attacks

Copyright © 2002 by Russell Pond. All rights reserved.
http://www.seasonofpeace.com

Written by Russell Pond
Edited by Amy Jennings Adams

ISBN 978-1480254657

Cover Design: Sovrenti Studios (http://www.sovrenti.com)
Cover Photo: Russell Pond

To my first true love,
Jesus Christ.
Apart from you, Lord,
I can do nothing.

CONTENTS

FOREWORD: WHAT IS ANXIETY DISORDER?

A lmost everyone suffers from nervousness at some time or another—prom night, final exams, job interviews. Likewise, few of us are immune to the flash of fear as we slam on our brakes and grip the steering wheel waiting for the impact of a stranger's car. Scientists refer to that rush of adrenaline as our "fight or flight" response. However, when anxiety takes control of your life, that adrenaline trigger can become overly sensitive causing fear and panic over everyday events like a pat on the back, a telephone call or an intrusive thought.

Anxiety disorders are the most common of emotional disorders, affecting more than 23 million Americans annually—that's approximately one in nine! Anxiety disorders include generalized anxiety disorder, phobias, obsessive-compulsive disorder, posttraumatic stress disorder, and panic disorder. Persistent physical and emotional symptoms—such as overwhelming feelings of fear, uncontrollable obsessive thoughts and rituals, flashbacks and/or nightmares, and puzzling physical sensations—often accompany these disorders. And, unlike normal feelings of nervousness, these symptoms often occur for no apparent reason. If left untreated, anxiety disorders can virtually immobilize sufferers, reducing productivity, devastating relationships, and turning everyday experiences into terrifying tasks.[1]

The American Psychiatric Association defines a panic attack as an unprovoked surge of fear. When panic strikes, symptoms spark "like the current in a cross-wired fire alarm: the heart races, breathing gets

---

[1] *Let's Talk Facts About: Anxiety Disorders*, American Psychiatric Association. Washington, D.C., © 1988 (revised 1997).

shallower and faster, the whole nervous system signals: **Danger!**" A person may be diagnosed with panic disorder if they suffer one or more of these panic attacks a month and experience at least four of the following symptoms:

- shortness of breath or smothering sensation
- heart palpitations or chest pain
- excessive sweating
- hot or cold flashes
- tingling or numbness
- trembling or shaking
- dizziness or lightheadedness
- nausea or abdominal distress
- feelings of detachment from reality
- fear of losing control, dying, or "going crazy"[1]

In fact, studies by the National Institute for Mental Health show that 25 to 30 percent of the people who go to the emergency room for chest pain or "heart problems" are really suffering from the results of a panic attack.

Agoraphobia often sets in as these attacks occur more frequently, and the victim begins to avoid places or situations where past episodes have occurred, the grocery store or shopping mall, for example.

If the above descriptions sound all too familiar to you or to someone you know, talk to your doctor or pastor. Don't be afraid to seek medical attention and wise counsel. With the help of the Great Physician guiding each of your steps, you will find your pathway to peace.

---

[1] *Let's Talk Facts About: Panic Disorder*, American Psychiatric Association. Washington, D.C., © 1988 (revised 1997).

INTRODUCTION

The early morning sun peered from behind a cloud as I headed towards San Antonio to finish a job. I had made the 45-minute drive many times before, but this Saturday morning was quite different.

As the skyline came into view, I noticed that my heart began to pound in my chest. I struggled to breathe—I couldn't seem to get enough air. *What's happening to me?* My hands and legs felt numb. *This is a heart attack!* My mind began to race. *I must be losing my mind!* I thought I was going to die. *Oh Lord,* I cried out, *please don't let me die!*

As it turned out, I didn't have a heart attack. I didn't go crazy, and I'm still alive to tell you about what I went through. I experienced what doctors call a panic attack.

As a child, these intense episodes were common. At night, I would lie in bed trying to rationalize "deep" issues like death and eternity. These thoughts triggered waves of terror. Shards of unreality stabbed at my mind. I ran screaming to my mom knowing she could calm the fears.

As I grew through the years, so did the fear. I tried to explain it to doctors, but most of them simply said my symptoms were the result of excess stress. "Russell, you worry too much," they would advise. "You just need to relax." If I were to write down the number of times someone said that to me, I could fill hundreds of pages.

In college, I discovered an effective form of self-medication—alcohol. At nights, when the anxiety was at its worst, my drinking temporarily numbed the fear. Without realizing what was happening, I

3

began to drink more and more. Nighttime binges became routine. Soon the alcohol controlled me.

During my senior year in college, my mom insisted that I see a psychiatrist. At our first meeting, the young doctor pulled out a large medical book. He handed me the giant publication and instructed me to read a section entitled *Chronic Panic Anxiety Disorder.*

I was shocked! This indescribable fear had a name—usually called *panic disorder* or *anxiety disease.* I sat there astonished as I read through the symptoms: racing heart, rapid breathing, feelings of unreality, thoughts of dying or going crazy. What a relief! I learned that I was not the only one who battled this problem.

The doctor prescribed an anti-anxiety medication, which provided some relief, but the fear continued...along with the drinking. As time passed, the fear built up to a point where I was afraid to be alone or to drive anywhere by myself—*agoraphobia,* I later learned, is a common companion of panic disorder.

After graduation, I accepted a job in Fort Worth. The loneliness of a new city and the pressures of a new profession pushed me deeper into despair. The torment of fear left me wanting to die. Yet, the fear of death, ironically, kept me alive. Torn between peace and panic, right and wrong, life and death, I cried out to God for answers. In utter hopelessness, I prayed a simple prayer, "God, if you are real, then you can help me. You can take away this fear."

I visited many churches. On my third visit to one particular church, the pastor began speaking about the fear he had faced. I had heard many people talk about fear before, but this man had my full attention. I knew the kind of fear he described.

When we met for the first time, he asked me to describe my experience. As I stumbled for words, he came to my rescue, saying, "Better yet, let me explain it to you." As he began to paint a picture of the panic, I could hardly believe it—he described to me my own fears.

Not only had this pastor experienced what I was experiencing, but he had found freedom from the fear. There was hope. For the first time in my life, I could see Light at the end of the tunnel.

That day, I embarked on a quest . . . a quest to learn as much as possible about panic disorder. I read books by doctors, psychiatrists, and psychologists who understand this anxiety disease. I collected every article I could find on the subject. I met and talked with other panic sufferers. I searched the Bible for all references to fear.

Yet, in all of my research, I could not find the overnight cure I so desperately sought. I longed for a "magic pill," but there was none to be found. So, I prayed. I searched. I begged for that one-time, spiritual zap that would forever set me free. It never came.

One day my wife said, "Do you know what I think? I think you will have those unwanted thoughts for the rest of your life. You just need to learn how to overcome them." It was a painful, but honest, revelation. Seeing the truth in her words, I came to a life-changing conclusion: God does not come into our lives to take away our problems; rather, he gives us the strength to overcome them.

Somewhat reluctantly, I accepted that healing is often a process—the time of recovery is typically related to the length of the disorder. For those who have been experiencing panic attacks for only a few years, freedom often comes within a few months, maybe even weeks. For others, like me, who have wrestled with this fear their entire life, the pathway to peace may be longer.

Each person's road to recovery is a unique one. For some, it can be a single step of faith bringing instant freedom and deliverance. For others, it's a journey. A journey of learning, trusting, growing and walking. It's an expedition of experience conforming us into his image.

The good news is that the Lord walks with us every step of the way, no matter where our path may take us. These devotions are a collection of the truths he has revealed to me along this journey of mine. You will learn more of my story as you read these pages; but far greater, I pray that you will learn more about your worth in Christ and about the love your Father longs to lavish on you.

Since I have had panic attacks all my life, I never really knew mental freedom. It wasn't until I placed all of my trust in Jesus Christ that I began to see the sunrise of a new season in my life—the *season of peace.*

If panic has become a part of your life, if you would like to begin your "season of peace," pray this simple prayer:

Father, I come to you defeated by this fear. I have tried to fight this battle alone, but I have failed. Forgive me. I realize that I am a sinner in the midst of a fallen, sinful world. Even though I did not deserve it, you sent your only Son to die on a cross in order to pay the debt for my sin. Yet, he rose to life on the third day, victorious over death. I will trust in you, Father. Help me to trust you even more, for you are greater than all my fears. Amen.

INSPIRATIONAL MESSAGES

*Be strong in your faith. Remember that
your Christian brothers and sisters all
over the world are going through the same
kind of suffering you are.*
1 Peter 5:9b, NLT

*And let us not grow weary while doing
good, for in due season we shall reap
if we do not lose heart.*
Galatians 6:9, NKJV

HIDING FROM YOUR FATHER

The story of Adam and Eve gives us the first account of fear recorded in the Bible. As most of you know, Eve was tempted by the "serpent" to disobey God's command. Adam, "who was with her," also ate some of the forbidden fruit.

Before the fall of man, God would walk with Adam and Eve in the garden. It was a time of fellowship. A time of communion. A time of intimacy. However, this one morning was quite different:

"Then the man and his wife heard the sound of the LORD God as he was walking in the garden in the cool of the day, and they hid from the LORD God among the trees of the garden."[1]

For their entire existence, Adam and Eve had experienced intimacy with God. They enjoyed true fellowship with the Almighty, the Creator of the Universe. He was their Father, and they were his children. But on this one day, something was different. They hid from their Father.

God called out to them, "Where are you?"

Adam answered, "I heard you in the garden, and I was afraid because I was naked; so I hid."[2]

Look at the four statements Adam made: I heard you. I was afraid. I was naked. I hid. The four results of disobeying God are:

- Conviction. (I heard you.)
- Fear. (I was afraid.)
- Shame. (I was naked.)
- Separation. (I hid.)

Please understand, I am not saying everyone's panic and fear is a direct result of some sin in your life. But, I do believe that fear is a result of being separated from God—a broken fellowship.

So, how do we restore fellowship with God? How do we walk with him and talk with him?

The first step is to confess your sins to Jesus; ask him to forgive you. He is faithful and ready to forgive you of your sins and cleanse you from all unrighteousness.[3] Then, spend some time praying and worshipping the Lord. If each one of us would spend quality time

8

with God, then his love would break down all the walls that separate us from him.

POINTS TO PONDER

1. Take a moment and pray the prayer below. Make a list of any sins that come to mind.
2. Do these sins make you feel afraid, ashamed or separated from God?
3. Have you ever tried to "hide" from God? If so, how?

PRAYER

Father, I know that if I confess my sins, you are faithful and just to forgive me. Thank you that because of your Son, Jesus, I no longer need to feel afraid or ashamed. Remove the wall that separates me from your peace, so that I may walk with you in the cool of the garden.

[1] Genesis 3:8, [2] 9b-10, NIV
[3] 1 John 1:9, paraphrased

Notes:
_____
_____
_____
_____
_____
_____
_____
_____
_____
_____

THE SPLINTER

When talking to people about panic attacks and root issues, I find myself using a common analogy: a splinter in your finger.

There are many ways we can deal with the pain of a splinter. We can numb the pain with ice. We can cover the splinter with bandages so that it won't be exposed. We can learn not to bend our finger a certain way that causes the pain.

Sometimes that splinter will fester into an infection causing more pain and more restricted movement. If nothing is done, the infection can spread, leading to even more serious problems.

Ideally, the best solution is to dig out the splinter. This brings up memories as a child when my mom would get a needle, a match and some alcohol. She would burn the end of the needle to sterilize it. Then, she'd get the alcohol ready to clean the hole she gouged in my finger. As a kid, I knew it was going to hurt.

Yes, there may be some pain in cutting out that splinter. Yes, there will even be some time required for proper healing. And yes, there may even be a scar. But, ultimately, the splinter will be gone. You will be able to move again without any pain, without any fear.

For most sufferers, panic disorder has a splinter. Root issues deep in our soul can trigger fear and panic. I believe one of my root issues was an inability to trust God, leading to a fear of death. For years, I anesthetized my pain by drinking. I covered the pain with the bandages of perfectionism. My splinter was buried deep in my soul, yet it continued to cause problems in my daily life and the lives of those close to me.

"See to it that no one misses the grace of God and that no bitter root grows up to cause trouble and defile many."[1]

Today, I encourage you to seek God for clarity about any splinters in your life. Trust him even when he burns the needle and grabs the alcohol. The pain of removing the splinter will be your first step towards healing. True freedom is within reach for everyone. God is ready to start work.

POINTS TO PONDER

1. Do you think there might be a "splinter" at the root of your fear and anxiety? If so, do you know what that "splinter" might be?
2. In what ways have you attempted to numb, bandage or adapt to this "splinter"?
3. Will you trust God to remove the "splinter," even if it might hurt a little in the process?

PRAYER

Father, the roots of my anxiety run deep. I have tried to deal with the pain in my own ways, but nothing has helped. I ask you to remove any "splinters" from my life, understanding that it may be a long and painful process. I trust you to bring healing where the "splinters" once pierced my heart.

[1] Hebrews 12:15, NIV

Notes:
_____
_____
_____
_____
_____
_____
_____
_____
_____
_____

A SEED OF HOPE

A knot formed in the pit of my stomach. I had sat in numerous counseling offices throughout my life. This time seemed no different. This was probably just another "session" of hopelessness and letdowns.

As I sat there, I wondered about the questions this gentleman would probably ask. Would he ask me to recount my childhood? Would he want me to describe my emotions during an attack? Would he ask me to dig up those painful memories that I spent years trying to bury? That knot in my stomach tightened.

Over the years, doctors and counselors interrogated me with hundreds of questions. "Tell me more about how you feel," they would urge. Their empty claims of "I understand" quickly lost their meaning. After all, if doctors and counselors could not explain these episodes of terror, then surely I was losing my mind.

"Russell," the gentleman began, "I know exactly what you are going through. You see, I've had panic attacks for more than 40 years." Immediately, this man had my attention.

"For years I couldn't drive anywhere. I couldn't sleep at nights. My world had closed in so much that my life really had no meaning. I was afraid of living, and I was afraid of dying."

Something inside me leapt. Anticipation quickly replaced that pit in my stomach as I listened to someone who knew exactly what I was experiencing. Then he continued, "And know this, that after 40 years of panic attacks, I am now completely free."

I sat there astonished. In a matter of minutes, I had gone from total despair to an overwhelming sense of hope. Hope that I could one day be free from this. Hope that I could one day live a normal, peaceful life.

That day brought a new beginning in my life. A seed of hope had been planted in my heart—a seed that God would begin to nurture and grow.

"What is faith? It is the confident assurance that what we hope for is going to happen. It is the evidence of things we cannot yet see."[1]

That seed of hope produced faith. I imagined a future not limited by fear—a future where I could grow and experience life to its fullest, a future full of peace and confidence.

POINTS TO PONDER

1. Have you ever reached a point where you almost gave up hope? Describe the situation and how you felt.
2. Describe the future for which you long.
3. Have you had an experience similar to the one I described where something or someone gave you a seed of hope? If so, describe.

PRAYER

Father, nurture and grow the seed of hope you have placed in my heart, cultivate it into the fruit of faith that I may be certain of a hopeful future.

[1] Hebrews 11:1, NLT

Notes:

_____
_____
_____
_____
_____
_____
_____
_____
_____
_____

PROMISES, PROMISES

God came to Abraham in a vision and told him, "Look toward heaven, and count the stars if you are able to number them. So shall your descendants be."[1]

Years passed, and still there were no children. Abraham was 99 years old. Sarah was 90. Could they still have a child at this age? Sarah laughed at the prospect. The odds were certainly against them.

What if I don't have this child God promised? What if I fail God? What if I die and there is no heir? What if . . . ? What if . . . ? Abraham could have listened to all those doubts and become downcast and distressed.

"Yet [Abraham] did not waver through unbelief regarding the promise of God, but was strengthened in his faith and gave glory to God, being fully persuaded that God had power to do what he had promised."[2]

I want to persuade you that God has the power to do what he has promised you. He may not come to you in a vision or a dream. He may not speak to you in a thundering voice. But, we do have promises through Jesus Christ. Here are some of those promises that you can stand on:

- "Never will I leave you; never will I forsake you."[3]
- Jesus said, "I give them eternal life, and they shall never perish; neither shall anyone snatch them out of My hand."[4]
- Jesus said, "In my Father's house are many rooms; if it were not so, I would have told you. I am going there to prepare a place for you."[5]
- Jesus said, "Peace I leave with you; my peace I give you."[6]

You can stand on these promises. God is more than able to do what he has promised you through Jesus. I encourage you to rest in these truths.

14

POINTS TO PONDER

1. When God doesn't answer your prayers exactly how and when you expect him to, do you ever lose faith?
2. Have you ever given up on God's promises? Have you ever questioned his goodness?
3. Make a list of some promises, no matter how big or small, for which you can trust God. If you do not know any of God's promises, spend some time reading the Bible and seeking God for the promises he has for you.

PRAYER

    Father, Abraham did not waver through unbelief because of your promises for him. Fear and panic come as a result of wavering in the storms of doubt. Help me to realize and see the promises you have for me. Then, give me the courage and strength to stand on those promises.

[1] Genesis 15:5, paraphrased
[2] Romans 4:20-21, NIV
[3] Hebrews 13:5b, NIV
[4] John 10:28, NKJV
[5] John 14:2, NIV
[6] John 14:27, NIV

Notes:
_____
_____
_____
_____
_____
_____
_____
_____
_____
_____

15

DYING TO OUR DESIRES

I have been crucified with Christ; it is no longer I who live, but Christ lives in me; and the life which I now live in the flesh I live by faith in the Son of God, who loved me and gave himself for me."[1]

Being crucified with Christ is such a hard concept to grasp. Yet, learning to die to ourselves is the key to life in Christ, a life full of peace.

Let's continue with our story of Abraham. God fulfilled his promise, and Sarah gave birth to Isaac. Can you imagine the hopes, the expectations, the dreams that Abraham had for his son? *This is my promised seed from God,* Abraham must have thought proudly. *Through him, thousands upon thousands of people will fill the earth.* A proud father. A confident patriarch.

Then, God commanded something that might seem totally contrary to his character: "Abraham, take your son, your only son, and offer him as a burnt offering."[2]

What? Kill my one and only son? Kill this promise you have fulfilled? Kill my hopes, my expectations, my dreams? The thoughts must have flooded Abraham's mind.

Yet, Abraham put aside his human reasoning and obeyed God's command. After he had laid Isaac on the altar and had raised a knife to kill him, an angel of the Lord stopped him. In the thicket, Abraham saw a ram that God had provided for him to sacrifice instead.

God wants us to die to our own desires, our own dreams. By dying to these desires, we are telling God that we fully trust him—that he knows what's best for us. God honored Abraham's obedience. God will honor your obedience. When we give up control of our own lives and are willing to die to ourselves, God will provide what we need. He can be trusted.

16

POINTS TO PONDER

1. Are you willing to be crucified in Christ? Have you truly died to your dreams and desires?
2. Can you recall a time when you have given up what you wanted in order to do what God wanted? What was the outcome of that decision?
3. Has God asked you to sacrifice some dreams, some hopes, some expectations? Is there anything in your life to which you are clinging, unwilling to let go? Write down anything you feel you need to surrender to God.

PRAYER

Father, if there is any area of my life, which I have not released to you, please show me. Reveal any part of my fleshly self that is still alive and needs to die. Help me to surrender my selfish desires to you, nailing them to the Cross. I will trust that you know what is best for me.

[1] Galatians 2:20, NKJV
[2] Genesis 22:2, paraphrased

Notes:

_____
_____
_____
_____
_____
_____
_____
_____
_____
_____

17

KEEPING A PROMISE

In today's society, a person's promise has lost its power. Contracts and legal documents have replaced promises. No more handshakes. No more verbal agreements. Why? Because so many people have come to a place where they cannot trust a person's word—a person's promise.

A few months ago, I was having some work done on my car. I wanted to pick it up before they closed, but I didn't have my checkbook. I couldn't pay until the next day. I thought, *I wonder if they'd let me have my car now and take my word that I will pay tomorrow?* Then, I had to laugh, *Yeah, right!*

Why is that? Has the world become so hardened to the power of a promise? Probably. Does that mean everyone breaks his or her promises? No.

But the world tells us, "No one can be trusted—not even God."

Promises are only as dependable as the character of the person making the promise. If Jesus had some car work done in your shop and asked you if he could take the car home now and pay tomorrow, could you trust him?

If God promises you that he will take care of you, can you trust him? I challenge you today to trust God with all your heart.[1] Trust him with something for which you've never trusted him before. Maybe it's finances. Maybe it's going to the shopping mall for the first time in years. Whatever it is, trust him. Let him reveal his faithfulness to you.

God keeps his promises.

"For no matter how many promises God has made, they are 'Yes' in Christ."[2]

18

POINTS TO PONDER

1. Have you ever been promised something only to be let down by a broken promise?
2. Have you ever made someone a promise but were unable to fulfill it?
3. Review the list of God's promises you have been making. Next to the ones God has fulfilled, write down when he fulfilled it.

PRAYER

Father, help me to trust your promises. Help me to see that your promises are "yes" and "amen" in Jesus' name! Show me that you can be trusted when you make a promise.

[1] Proverbs 3:5
[2] 2 Corinthians 1:20a, NIV

Notes: _____

_____

_____

_____

_____

_____

_____

_____

_____

_____

TRACKING DOWN THE TRUTH

Fear has a way of making us believe things that are not true. Panic attacks epitomize this. For more than 20 years, I was convinced that I was going crazy or had some terrible, life-threatening disease. Yet, this was not true. For more than 20 years, I believed a lie. Let me share another story about a man who believed a lie for more than 20 years.

Jacob was a proud father. His twelve sons must have brought him tremendous joy. There was one son, though, of whom he was most proud. His son, Joseph. He was so proud of this young son, that he made a special robe for him—a robe of many colors. That gift to Joseph represented his father's favor.

The older brothers were jealous of Joseph, and decided to get rid of him. In a fit of envy, they sold Joseph to some Midianite traders. To cover their wickedness, they took his special robe and doused it with the blood of a goat. When they went back to their father, they handed it to him and said, "We found this. Examine it to see whether it is your son's robe."[1]

Immediately, Jacob cried out in misery, "It is my son's robe! Some ferocious animal has devoured him. Joseph has surely been torn to pieces."[2] His favorite son was gone, or so he thought. He simply saw the evidence, and believed a lie.

Years passed, and Joseph became governor over all Egypt. During the famine, his brothers came seeking food. They did not recognize their younger brother. But, after a few discussions with them, Joseph eventually revealed himself to them.

When the older brothers went back to tell their father that Joseph was still alive—to tell him the truth—Jacob could not believe it.[3] Eventually, Jacob did learn that Joseph was alive. But for more than 20 years, Jacob believed a lie.

When panic strikes, the evidence seems very real. Something must be terribly wrong—a rapid heart beat, shallow breathing, numbing hands, pain, terror. Yet, we do nothing to track down the truth. We simply accept that the evidence is real.

How long have you believed the evidence?

Today, I encourage you to track down the truth. Had Jacob investigated this story of an attack, he might have learned the truth and

20

saved himself years of anguish. Ask God to help you find the truth. Once you find it, **"then you will know the truth, and the truth will set you free."**[4]

POINTS TO PONDER

1. Have you, past or present, listened to the lies of panic and anxiety?
2. Have you ever believed you were having a heart attack? Have you believed your condition was because of some terrible, life-threatening disease? How long have you believed these lies?
3. Have you asked God to reveal the truth to you? In what ways can you track down the truth?

PRAYER

Father, I will no longer believe the lies of my enemy. Reveal to me the truth, O Lord, your truth and love that I may believe and be set free. Give me the strength and courage I need to "track down the truth" whether it's physical or spiritual, past or present, real or perceived.

[1] Genesis 37:32, [2] 33, NIV
[3] Genesis 45:26
[4] John 8:32, NIV

Notes: _____

_____

_____

_____

_____

_____

_____

_____

_____

_____

BROKENNESS

Whaen I think of a person who has experienced the terror, the pain, the bondage of crippling anxiety, one word comes to mind: brokenness. Brokenness is a place where all human effort is shattered.

A place where hope becomes the only source of strength.

A place where the foundation of faith will be tested.

A place where there is no one to trust but God himself.

I love the story of Joseph. His life exemplifies brokenness. As a young lad, he was rejected by his brothers, sold as a slave and held in prison for years. Why? Because he shared his dreams, his God-given dreams.

Can you imagine what must have gone through his mind throughout all those years? "Why me? What have I done to deserve this pain, this suffering?" Yet, even in prison, Joseph held on to his integrity. When approached and seduced by Potiphar's wife, he held fast to his convictions and ran away, risking death and more suffering for the sake of righteousness.

As Joseph continued serving the Lord with a pure heart, God exalted him, raising him to the position of steward over the prison. During this time, he interpreted the dreams of two men who served Pharaoh. Then, two years later he was called before Pharaoh to interpret the king's troublesome nightmares. After successfully interpreting the dreams, Joseph was placed second in command over all of Egypt.

Joseph's brokenness opened a door for God's hand of blessing and provision—not only for Joseph, but for his entire family as well.

"The sacrifices of God are a broken spirit. A broken and contrite heart, O God, you will not despise."[1]

Joseph's life—full of pain and rejection—was a sacrifice. Brokenness is far from a pleasant experience. In fact, it is very painful. But, only when a vessel is broken can light shine through the cracks. God does not reject a broken and contrite heart. Your brokenness can also be a sacrifice to God.

22

POINTS TO PONDER

1. Is your heart broken? If so, list some of the assaults and afflictions that have led to this brokenness.
2. Often we try to patch the cracks of our hearts with the temporary glue of this world. In what ways have you done this?
3. Have you, like Joseph, offered your broken heart to the Lord as a sacrifice? Have you continued to serve him with integrity throughout your pain?

PRAYER

Father, I have been hurt by others and by my own actions and decisions. My heart aches like a broken bone, which has not yet mended. I realize that I cannot put the pieces back together—forgive me for even trying. I offer these pieces to you as a sacrifice. Do with my heart as you will.

[1] Psalm 51:17, NIV

Notes:
_____
_____
_____
_____
_____
_____
_____
_____
_____
_____

STAND STILL

Moses and the Israelites had just marched out of Egypt when they approached the Red Sea. Some of the families in the back noticed a large cloud of dust rising over the hills behind them—Pharaoh and his army! With mountains on both sides, a sea in front and danger racing towards them, the people were struck with fear.

"Did you bring us here to die in the desert?" the people cried out.[1] But the Lord spoke to Moses, and Moses answered the people, **"Don't be afraid. Just stand where you are and watch the Lord rescue you."**[2]

The natural response to fear is to either run from or fight those horrible feelings. Yet, God calls us to go beyond our natural response—he calls us to *stand still*.

I remember my first key victory over panic attacks. I was sitting in a recliner holding my three-month-old son at my in-laws. Fear gripped me. My body went numb. My heart raced, pounding uncontrollably—I had been trapped in this Red Sea valley before.

In the past, I fought the fear with all my strength. I ran. I screamed. I did everything in my power to alleviate the anxiety. It never worked. Weary from past struggles, I had no strength left to fight. This time, I remained still. I prayed, "Lord, I am going to trust you and not fight these fearful thoughts."

After a few minutes, I noticed that the fear had passed. I was amazed. No fear! *Thank you Lord*, I thought. Then I sensed his still, small voice say, "Russell, you trusted me."

When the Israelites stood still, God parted the Red Sea. When we stand still in the midst of our fear, we will see the miraculous salvation of God in our own lives. It's not easy to stand still when everything inside you screams, "Run!" But with God at your side, you can rest through anything.

24

POINTS TO PONDER

1. How do you respond to fearful thoughts or situations that make you anxious?
2. What do you think God means by *stand still*? What does that mean to you?
3. Have you ever tried to "be still" in the midst of a panic attack? Next time, give it a try.

PRAYER

Father, help me to stand still when fear arises. When I am faced with an anxious situation, give me the strength to rest in your promises and trust you. Fill me with courage to be still and know that you are God.[3]

[1] Exodus 14:11, paraphrased
[2] Exodus 14:13a, NLT
[3] Psalm 46:10a, paraphrased

Notes: _____

_____
_____
_____
_____
_____
_____
_____
_____
_____

BUSYNESS

In a world of email and Internet, faxes and Federal Express, we have become a very busy people. Our minds are constantly being bombarded from so many directions, creating in us a sense of urgency.

Busyness, for many, can actually be just as numbing as a drug or stiff drink. With our minds so distracted with doing things, we can easily stuff those anxious thoughts into a mental drawer to deal with later, with hopes of them just going away altogether. Yet, the consequences of our busyness create a never-ending cycle of anxiety.

Is it possible to slow down and "smell the roses"? I believe it is. The distraction of busyness has been my anesthesia for many years. Even as I write this, I'm on a plane returning to Dallas from a business trip. I'll go back to work for a couple of days, while spending my evenings shooting video for a television show. On top of all that, I have to prepare for my trip to Germany on Monday.

While I don't think it is wrong to be busy, an overloaded schedule with unbalanced priorities can be unhealthy--physically and mentally.

Is there hope? Is there a solution? If I, Mr. Daytimer, can "still myself" in the bedlam of my busyness, then I know you can as well. In fact, I believe God calls us to be still. It is in that stillness that he "speaks" to our hearts and gives us a peace that passes all understanding. Listen for God's heart on this subject:

"You will keep him in perfect peace whose mind is stayed on You, because he trusts in You."[1]

"Be still before the Lord, and wait patiently for him."[2]

"My soul finds rest in God alone; my salvation comes from him."[3]

Peace really is possible. Don't let the busyness of life steal from you. Don't let it take your time with God or your peace of mind. Slow down and rest. If you have to, schedule it. Make time to "be still", and let the Lord "quiet you with his love."[4]

POINTS TO PONDER

1. Have you ever felt like God has taken you to a place where there is nothing to do but wait on him? Describe that "place."
2. What does it mean to you to "be still" before God? Do you find it hard to do?
3. Write down some practical ways you can be still, physically and mentally.

PRAYER

Father, teach me to wait on you. Help me to be still in the midst of a fast-paced world. I want to rest in you—in your arms of peace.

[1] Isaiah 26:3, NKJV
[2] Psalms 37:7, NIV
[3] Psalm 62:1, NIV
[4] Zephaniah 3:17, NIV

Notes: _____

_____
_____
_____
_____
_____
_____
_____
_____
_____

CONFESSIONS OF AN ADRENALINE JUNKIE

Adrenaline. I love the stuff. I feed off of it. Thriving. Striving. I drive myself hard. I press on despite the stress, the damage, the unhealthy effects on my mind and body. I'll be the first to admit it: I'm an adrenaline junkie.

Deadlines approaching. Projects promised. Relatives call with last-minute plans to visit. Things need to get done. Someone has got to take control, and I will do it! Those excessive demands can be met. I've got to push myself. With the adrenal glands in overdrive, the decisions are quick, accurate, split-second precise. Ah, yes! Progress.

Slow down? You've got to be kidding. I don't have time. I've got things to do, people to see. Resting is for wimps.

Two years ago, we spent Christmas in a small, dairy community located high atop the Swiss Alps. It was terribly small—no cars, no trains, no buses. The hotel room had no phone, no television, no computer access. The sun rose at 8:30 am and set at 4:30 pm. Needless to say, things were moving way too slow for me.

As an adrenaline junkie, this turtle's pace was torment. I was so bored—pacing-the-room bored. I had to be doing something, anything. "Please, give me a project, a task, something to do!" my mind would scream.

Does any of this sound familiar? Are you an adrenaline junkie? Do you thrive on progress, achievement and accomplishment? Are you easily frustrated when something or someone impedes your progress? Take this simple test: sit down and do nothing. No reading, no praying, no sleeping, no television, no computer. Nothing. How long can you do that? You may be surprised at the results.

Adrenaline can be good, even life-saving. This God-given hormone helps us in threatening situations, giving us a quick, accurate response when faced with an emergency. But, the prolonged and improper use of this natural "fight or flight" intensity can be dangerous, creating terrible anxiety and panic attacks.

When it comes to adrenaline-induced energy, is it really worth it? Are you willing to sacrifice your physical and mental health for sake of a project, a deadline, a pat on the back? Is it really worth it?

Each day, I'm learning to rest a little more. Even during my holiday vacation in Switzerland, I was able slow down, sleep in and

28

rest. Balance is becoming more and more important in my daily routine. And with that balance comes peace—peace that passes all understanding.

I want to encourage you with one scripture, a command from the Lord: **"Be still and know that I am God."** [1]

POINTS TO PONDER

1. Would you consider yourself an adrenaline junkie? Why? Why not?
2. How did you do on the "simple test"? Describe your results.
3. What can you do to slow down? List some practical examples.

PRAYER

Father, help me to slow down and rest in you. Reveal to me any fast-paced area of my life that is beyond healthy. Show me how to slow down. Show me how I can rest in your promises.

[1] Psalm 46:10a, NKJV

Notes: _____

_____

_____

_____

_____

_____

_____

_____

_____

_____

WANDERING THROUGH THE WILDERNESS

The wilderness. For forty years, the children of Israel wandered around in the wilderness. What could have taken 11 days, took four decades.

When I think of the wilderness, I think of a dry, barren place. A place where there is no refreshing water, no cool breeze—no life.

In many ways, I see fear and panic disorder like a wilderness. A place in our heart where there is no life, no growth—only a painful hot wind that scorches the joy from our lives.

When I first became a Christian, I used to cry out to God, "Lord, please help me out of this wilderness of fear and doubt." For a while, I studied the children of Israel and their trek through this arid place. As I searched and searched for a reason why these people wandered for 40 years, I came across this scripture:

"Remember how the LORD your God led you all the way in the desert these forty years, to humble you and to test you in order to know what was in your heart, whether or not you would keep his commands. He humbled you, causing you to hunger and then feeding you with manna, which neither you nor your fathers had known, to teach you that man does not live on bread alone but on every word that comes from the mouth of the LORD."[1]

The Israelites' experience in the desert was a time of testing, a time of training, a time of transformation. The Lord was teaching his children how to trust in him, how to feed off of every word that comes from his mouth.

Do you remember why they were sentenced to 40 years in the desert? When the people heard about the giants in the land, they did not trust that the Lord would give them victory. They doubted. They came to the "Promised" Land, yet they did not believe in God's promise.

Let me encourage you that there is a Promised Land:

A land of peace.

A land of growth.

A land of joy.

A land of rest.

A land of abundance.

Trust God. He will give you victory over the giants of fear and panic. He will go before you and defeat the enemy. Put your trust in

30

him, and he will deliver you, "so that in the end it might go well with you."[2]

POINTS TO PONDER

1. Is your heart dry and barren from years of fear? Is there little growth, little joy, little life?
2. Do you think it is possible that God is humbling you, testing you to see whether or not you will keep his commandments? List some specific ways you intend to keep God's commandments.
3. Do you trust God to deliver you from anxiety? Why, or why not?

PRAYER

Father, I humble myself before you that I may not doubt your strength as the Israelites did. I trust you to guide me to the Promised Land of peace.

[1] Deuteronomy 8:2-3, NIV
[2] Deuteronomy 8:16b, NIV

Notes:
_____
_____
_____
_____
_____
_____
_____
_____
_____
_____

THE PROMISED LAND OF PEACE

Moses and the children of Israel had wandered around in the wilderness and camped out in the desert long enough. The time had come for them to cross over into the Promised Land.

For 40 years, they had been fed heavenly bread called manna every morning. They didn't plant. They didn't harvest. God sent them nourishment supernaturally. Each day, they followed a cloud of glory by day and the fire of God by night. Each day, Moses would speak to God for the people, and God would speak to the people through Moses.

His provision . . .

His protection . . .

His presence . . .

. . . were obvious every day.

However, once this new generation of people crossed over the Jordan, there would be no more manna, no more fire by night or cloud by day. Moses would no longer speak to God for them. It represented a new era of his provision, protection and presence. The Israelites had to simply trust God in this new land of Promise.

Moses instructed the people, "Be strong and of good courage, do not fear nor be afraid of them; for the LORD your God, He is the One who goes with you. He will not leave you nor forsake you."[1]

These words ring true for everyone battling fear and panic. Our land of promise, our land of peace, lies before us. As we step across the river, there will be giants; there will be battles; there will even be set backs. We must be strong and of good courage. Why? Because God goes with us. He will not leave us nor forsake us.

Be of good courage for your Father goes with you.

32

POINTS TO PONDER

1. Are you so afraid of fighting the enemy, Fear, that you are wandering around in the wilderness instead of entering the Promised Land of peace?
2. What battles or challenges particularly frighten you? Going to the grocery store? Driving your car? Being alone?
3. Write down your definition of courage.

PRAYER

Father, I believe that you have prepared a place of peace for me. Help me to be strong and courageous, trusting that you will journey with me and fight the fear for me. Lead me to the Promised Land as you led the children of Israel.

[1] Deuteronomy 31:6, NKJV

Notes:
_____
_____
_____
_____
_____
_____
_____
_____
_____
_____

33

THE WALL OF WORRY

When the children of Israel were ready to enter the Promised Land, Joshua led them across the Jordan River to a city outside of Jericho.

Jericho—with its mammoth wall—stood before them. This would be their first battle. It looked like a lop-sided fight as a bunch of inexperienced Israelites headed into battle against a strong fortress of fighters.

As Joshua sought God on how to fight this battle, an angel with his sword drawn appeared before him. He gave Joshua specific instructions on how to fight. He explained that the people should walk around the city once a day for seven days. On the seventh day, they should walk around seven times. Afterwards, they should blow their trumpets and shout.

In faith, the Israelites walked quietly around the city just as Joshua commanded them to do. They couldn't say a word while marching. Then, on the seventh day after the seventh trip around, the people shouted and sounded the trumpets.

"When the trumpets sounded, the people shouted, and at the sound of the trumpet, when the people gave a loud shout, the wall collapsed; so every man charged straight in, and they took the city."[1]

Many times, I feel like the Israelites. No experience. No strength. No way I can fight against that fortress of fear. It's just too tall, too big.

The next time that tall wall of fear stands before you, call out to God. Ask him to show you how to bring those walls down.

Maybe it will be a shout of praise.

Maybe it will be a song in your heart.

Maybe it will be a confidence.

Whatever God tells you to do, do it. When you do, the walls will come tumbling down.

POINTS TO PONDER

1. Have you ever felt imprisoned by a wall of fear? How thick was this wall? How high?
2. Do you ever feel outnumbered by fears, doubts, worries, obsessions? Describe.
3. Have you tried to demolish the wall in your own strength? Describe the outcome.

PRAYER

Father, I am so weak and inexperienced. I cannot tear down this wall of fear on my own. Tell me what to do as I stand against my enemies. Give me the faith to wait on you and trust your promises.

[1] Joshua 6:20, NIV

Notes:
_____
_____
_____
_____
_____
_____
_____
_____
_____
_____

YESTERDAY'S VICTORY

The children of Israel had just defeated Jericho miraculously. Confidence was high. Morale was peaking. This new generation of warriors just experienced their first victory through God's wall-crumbling power.

The next battle in their path was the small city of Ai. After their reconnaissance, the spies advised Joshua to send out only a few men. It was an easy victory . . . or so they thought.

However, when they attacked the city, the Israelites were chased into retreat and defeated. The soldiers came back to Joshua beaten and bloodied. They couldn't overtake Ai. God was not with them.

Israel lost courage. Confusion and doubts began to rise up in their minds. Confidence hit an all time low.

What Joshua didn't realize was that someone in the camp had disobeyed God. Against God's command, Achan kept some of the spoil from the Jericho victory for himself and buried it under his tent. That disobedience kept the mighty men of Israel from defeating the small city of Ai.

After dealing with the sin, the Lord gave Joshua a new plan to defeat the small, but powerful city. With God's help, the Israelites destroyed Ai.

When I read this story, it reminds me of my own journey into the Promised Land of peace. One day, I experienced a miraculous victory over panic attacks. I trusted the Lord and rested through the attack. My confidence ran high. I was walking proud.

Like Joshua, though, I headed out presumptuously into the next day. Panic again pounced on my mind. Dismay and doubts came crashing in. *Where's God?* I thought. *Why isn't this working like it did yesterday?*

Instead of trusting God and getting his guidance for my next battle, I went out in the confidence of *my* strength and *my* power. Like Achan, I had kept the spoils of the last victory to myself.

God should be our guide through each battle we face regarding panic and fear. If we remove all sin from our lives, seek his guidance and obey his instructions, we will be victorious. We will take the Promised Land of peace.

"Give us aid against the enemy, for the help of man is worthless. With God we will gain the victory, and he will trample down our enemies."[1]

POINTS TO PONDER

1. Have you ever experienced the victory of overcoming a particular situation regarding panic attacks or fear? How long did that victory last?
2. Did you thank God for that victory?
3. Create a journal of your victories. Document your prayers and give glory to God for helping you through rough times. Then, seek his guidance for the next battle.

PRAYER

Father, thank you for every victory I have experienced in the past because I know they came only through you. Reveal to me the times when I "went out on my own strength" and failed. Teach me how to seek your guidance and direction each morning as I face the battlefield for that day.

[1] Psalm 60:11-12, NIV

Notes:
_____
_____
_____
_____
_____
_____
_____
_____
_____
_____

THE FACADE OF FEAR

News of Jericho and Ai had spread throughout the land. The surrounding kings and people had also heard of the Lord's miracles. They knew this was to be more than a physical battle.

The Hivites in Gibeon were among the local people who knew about these Hebrews. They were greatly afraid of Joshua for they knew that the children of Israel had come to take the land and destroy the inhabitants.

The Hivites knew they couldn't defeat Joshua and his God, so they formulated another plan. They donned some worn-out sacks for clothes. They loaded their oldest donkeys with moldy bread and old wineskins, and went to meet with Joshua.

"We have come from a distant country. Please make a treaty with us," pleaded the Hivites in disguise.

They had the appearance of foreigners from a distant land. Still, the men of Israel questioned them, "Perhaps you live near us. How then can we make a treaty with you?"

The delegation from Gibeon continued the masquerade. "This bread of ours was warm on the day we left. But see how dry and moldy it is now. And these wineskins that we filled were new, but see how cracked they are. And our clothes and sandals are worn out by the very long journey."[1]

"The men of Israel sampled their provisions but did not inquire of the LORD."[2]

They were duped. They fell for the moldy-bread-and-old-wineskin trick. They signed a treaty, thus disobeying God's command to destroy the Hivites.

Fear is like that. The wolf comes to you in sheep's clothing, bearing bogus gifts, creating a false impression. It has a way of making things seem one way when they are really another. It's a powerful bluff.

The men of Israel really only made one mistake. Did you catch it? They "did not inquire of the Lord."

God is ready for you to inquire of him. He wants to guide and lead you and expose the facade of fear.

POINTS TO PONDER

1. In what ways does fear disguise itself?
2. When the voice of fear speaks to your mind, do you recognize him as the enemy? Do you accept what he tells you as truth, or do you inquire of the Lord?
3. Make a list of truths that you can use to counter the lies of fear when it arises.

PRAYER

Father, enable me to recognize fear when it first approaches. Show me how to respond when I face fearful situations. Give me strength to stand, courage to continue, and grant me victory over fear.

[1] Joshua 9, paraphrased
[2] Joshua 9:14, NIV

Notes: _____

_____

_____

_____

_____

_____

_____

_____

_____

_____

GLASS JARS AND TRUMPETS

The Midianites had been cruel to the Israelites, destroying their crops, their homes, their families. In fact, the Israelites were so afraid of the Midianites that they fled to the mountains and hid in caves.

Yet, when Gideon was preparing to attack thousands upon thousands of Midianites, God spoke some specific instructions: **"You have too many warriors with you."**[1]

What? Too many warriors? Why does that matter?

"If I let all of you fight the Midianites, the Israelites will boast to me that they saved themselves by their own,"[2] **God explained.**

God gave Gideon one basic command: "Trust me." He was asking Gideon not to fight as he would naturally; rather, he was calling him to a supernatural battle—a battle fought by God, not by man.

After a couple of God-ordained tests, Gideon's army, which started out as 32,000 soldiers, stood at 300 men. Though his physical army seemed small, his heavenly army more than made up the difference.

With a trumpet in one hand and a glass jar in the other, Gideon's army of 300 surrounded the Midianite camp.

What? Glass jars and trumpets? Where were the swords and armor? Where were the archers to fire arrows into the camp? The chariots and horses to trample the enemy?

Again, God had other plans. He had selected Gideon and his small band of warriors as instruments to bring forth a supernatural victory—a victory for which only God could get the credit.

I have learned that my battle with fear and panic is similar in many ways. I can gather an army of psychiatrists, psychologists, medication, meditation, self-help books, support groups, breathing techniques, relaxation tapes and more. I might amass enough resources to beat this thing. But who gets the credit?

I believe God desires to instruct each person on which resources he wants to use in your battle. Maybe it's medication or a good counselor, or maybe it's a combination of both. Maybe it's something odd like glass jars and trumpets. Maybe God wants you to

40

fight this battle alone. Whatever God instructs you to do, do it. After all, this is *his* battle.

Each one of the resources I listed are powerful tools for healing and recovery when God works through them. However, you can't place your trust in your resources—your personal army against anxiety. Call upon God for guidance. Let him show you what he wants you to do.

POINTS TO PONDER

1. What "weapons" are you carrying into your battle against anxiety? Write them down.
2. Have you prayed about these and other resources? Do you feel peace in your heart about using these resources? Why or why not?
3. When you experience victory, to whom do you give credit? To your medication? To your doctor? To God?

PRAYER

Father, show me which "weapons," if any, you would have me carry. I praise you for past and future victories, because I know that only through your Son will I win this battle.

[1] Judges 7:2a, [2]b, NLT

Notes:

_____

_____
_____
_____
_____
_____
_____
_____
_____
_____
_____

41

FIGHTING GIANTS

One night, my wife and I were putting our son down for bed. We asked him, "What would you like for us to read tonight?" Since he was only two years old, we didn't expect a response. But he replied, "David."

With surprised looks on our faces, we opened up his toddlers' Bible to the story of David and Goliath. As we read, Caleb watched closely and listened carefully.

Afterwards, we crawled up into bed to say our prayers. Before we could start, Caleb sat up and said, "Daddy, I fight the giant."

I responded, "Okay," and placed my hand on his head praying, "Lord, I pray that you would strengthen Caleb to fight any giants in his life by trusting you for strength and victory. Amen."

Afterwards, Caleb paused, then looked at me and said, "Daddy, you fight the giant."

I said, "Okay, but you need to pray for me." So, he put his hand on my head and mumbled something followed by a loud "Amen!"

He sat there staring at me with a puzzled expression on his face. I could sense his little mind pondering this business of fighting giants. Then, he said, "Daddy, *we* fight the giant."

There is so much truth in the words of children. I realized that so many times in our life, we try to "fight the giant" by ourselves. Or, we call upon our Father to "fight the giant" for us.

Instead, we should look up to our Father and say, "Daddy, *we* fight the giant."

As Moses encouraged Joshua, **"Do not be afraid of them; the LORD your God himself will fight for you."**[1]

Together with our Father, we can overcome any giant in our life.

POINTS TO PONDER

1. What are some of the "giants" you face today?
2. In what ways do you try to fight these "giants" alone? Are you successful?
3. Have you ever asked for God's help in fighting these "giants"? If so, have you felt his strength, or sensed him fighting along with you?

PRAYER

Father, there are so many problems that hover over my life, threatening to destroy the peace and conquer the freedom I have in you. I know that you do not intend for me to fight these battles on my own. Fight with me, Lord. Fight for me, and allow me to feel the sweep of your mighty sword against the enemy on my behalf.

[1] Deuteronomy 3:22, NIV

Notes: _____
_____
_____
_____
_____
_____
_____
_____
_____
_____

SPIRITUAL SLINGSHOTS

My son's fascination for David-and-Goliath continued as we focused on the miraculous story throughout the week. Bedtime stories, color-book renderings, animated videos.

"Daddy, I want a slingshot," Caleb announced one day.

Using an old sock and two pieces of string, we created a makeshift slingshot. Grabbing an old tennis ball, I demonstrated how to place the ball in the old sock. Then, I swung it around and around strategically releasing one of the strings to catapult the ball through the air.

"Daddy, I do it. I do it." Caleb shouted.

Realizing that a tennis ball and old sock couldn't do too much damage to a two-year-old, I placed the ball in the slingshot, and handed it to Caleb. Mimicking the various stories we had read, Caleb shouted, "I will help save Israel!"

Around and around swished the old red sock. I was quite impressed. Then, it happened: the strings tangled in his arms, quickly wrapping around his hands. The tennis ball flipped round about and hit him in the back of the head. I couldn't hold back the laughter. He had tried so hard to fight the giant.

Then, he picked up the ball and said, "Daddy, I do it again." So, he pressed on, learning to use this newly discovered weapon.

I thought about Caleb's desire to learn about the natural weapons of this world. Then, I became grateful that we don't have natural weapons to fight our enemy. We have spiritual weapons— weapons that are powerful and mighty.

"For though we live in the world, we do not wage war as the world does. The weapons we fight with are not the weapons of the world. On the contrary, they have divine power to demolish strongholds. We demolish arguments and every pretension that sets itself up against the knowledge of God . . . ."[1]

"For our struggle is not against flesh and blood, but against the rulers, against the authorities, against the powers of this dark world and against the spiritual forces of evil in the heavenly realms. Therefore put on the full armor of God . . . ."[2]

Buckle the **belt of truth** around your waist.

Don the **breastplate of righteousness**.

44

Fit your **feet with the gospel of peace**.
Pick up the **shield of faith**.
Put on the **helmet of salvation**.
Take up the **sword of the Spirit**, the Word of God.[3]

Prepare yourself for battle against the enemies of fear and panic. With the spiritual armor in place, you are ready to do battle. You *will* be victorious!

POINTS TO PONDER

1. Have you ever been "hit in the head" while trying to fight the enemy with weapons of this world? Describe.
2. Read Ephesians 6:10-20 now. List each element of armor (noted in bold above), and explain how that piece can aid you in your spiritual battle.
3. Do you ever practice putting on the "full armor of God" by praying through this passage before you begin your day? If so, what results have you seen? If not, give it a try.

PRAYER

Father, thank you for providing this armor so that I may stand against the enemy. Remind me to clothe myself each morning with your strength so that I may defend myself from the fiery arrows of Satan's lies.

[1] 2 Corinthians 10:3-5a, NIV
[2] Ephesians 6:12-13a, NIV
[3] Ephesians 6:14-17, paraphrased

Notes:
_____
_____
_____
_____
_____
_____
_____
_____

ON GUARD

The other day, I went to see a movie with my brother and dad. It was one of those male-bonding, testosterone-inducing, action flicks. Shooting, explosions, body parts flying. Arrr!

Yet, when I walked out of the movie, my heart was racing with anxiety. The movie had put me on the edge of my seat and raised my adrenaline to an unhealthy level. I could feel my stomach churning as my hands started getting cold and tingly.

Before I went to the show, I was having a good day, full of peace and confidence. Yet afterwards, I was reaching for my anxiety medicine and facing the onslaught of anxious thoughts that were intruding into my mind.

So many worldly amusements are just not healthy for the mind:

The adultery and deception on television.

The flesh and lust in beer commercials.

The carnage and destruction in action movies.

Our hearts are very sensitive. That is how God created them—to be tender. Yet, as we pour the deceit of this world into our hearts, they grow hard and cold, callused to the sensitivity of God.

Proverbs wisely instructs us, **"above all else, guard your heart, for it is the wellspring of life."**[1]

You should carefully guard what is poured into the wellspring of your soul. Ask God to show anything that is not of him. Ask him to help you guard your heart.

POINTS TO PONDER

1. Carefully consider what you pour into your heart. Are there any unwholesome ideas that have penetrated the wellspring of your soul?
2. List any potentially unhealthy pastimes of which the Lord convicts you. (Watching a certain television program or reading certain types of books, for example.)
3. Are you willing to relinquish these activities? Would you be willing to relinquish them if your anxiety would subside?

PRAYER

Father, reveal to me anything in my heart that is not of you. Enable me to concentrate my time and energy on activities that will glorify you and bring peace to my life. Help me to guard my heart from anything that might contradict your Word or compete with your Lordship.

[1] Proverbs 4:23, NIV

Notes:
_____
_____
_____
_____
_____
_____
_____
_____
_____
_____

FEEDING THE FIRE

W hen I was a kid, my family went camping almost every weekend during the summer. We had such a great time water-skiing, fishing, roasting hot dogs and cooking hamburgers. I always wanted to make the campfires—after all, three years of Boy Scout training and the Fire Merit Badge shouldn't go to waste.

Meticulously, I would whittle slivers of wood into a small pile. Then, I would place smaller branches on top, slowly building up the pile of wood until it was ready to ignite.

As soon as the little pile of kindling would catch fire, there was still much more work left to do. As the embers began to glow, I would start blowing on the fire. To keep the embers from going out, I'd huff and puff and nearly pass out trying to get that fire started.

I always thought it strange that to feed the fire, you had to blow on it. You would think naturally that blowing on the fire would put it out. Rather, blowing on the fire feeds it with oxygen, causing the flames to burn hotter.

In many ways, panic attacks are the same. By fighting the fear, you are feeding the fire. When you focus your mind and your strength on fighting the panic attack, you are actually releasing more adrenaline causing the fear to rise up even stronger.

Think about it. Before that panic trigger strikes, your mind is off somewhere in thought. Life is peaceful. Then, that first symptom hits you. Your mind naturally concludes, "Oh no, I have to stop the panic from coming!" Now, you have directed your thoughts to one focal point: stop the fear. Your mind is focused on fighting the fear. You are blowing on the fire.

Claire Weekes talks about "floating the thought" in her book *Peace for the Nervous Sufferer.*[1] When that first thought comes, just let it come. Don't fight it. It hasn't killed you in the past. You haven't gone crazy.

As the Bible says, "It will come to pass." What that means is: it will come *and* it will pass. Put no strength into fighting the fear. Let God be your strength.

"My health may fail, and my spirit may grow weak, but God remains the strength of my heart; he is mine forever."[2]

POINTS TO PONDER

1. How do you "feed the fire" at the first sign of anxiety or a panic attack?
2. Have you ever tried "floating the thought"? If so, how did it work? If not, would you be willing to try?
3. List some practical ways in which you can refrain from fighting the fear. For example, you could close your eyes and try to relax or busy yourself with another activity.

PRAYER

Father, I am weak, but you are strong.[3] *The next time the enemy kindles fear within me, allow me to resist the temptation to "feed the fire," remaining calm as you reduce the blazing fire to ashes.*

[1] Weekes, Claire. *Peace from Nervous Suffering*. Signet (Penguin Books), New York City, 1990.
[2] Psalm 73:26, NLT
[3] 1 Corinthians 4:10b, paraphrased

Notes: _____
_____
_____
_____
_____
_____
_____
_____
_____
_____

DISCOURAGEMENT

In a land full of wickedness, where Ahab reigned with Queen Jezebel at his side, it had not rained in three and a half years. The prophet Elijah summoned 450 prophets of Baal and 400 prophets of Asherah to meet him on Mount Carmel. There he challenged them to choose a bull, place it on the altar and call down fire from their gods. "The god who answers—he is God."[1]

After the evil prophets chose their bull and prepared their sacrifice, they prayed for fire from heaven. There was no answer. No fire. No display of power. Hours went by. They were crying out, screaming to their gods, even cutting themselves. Nothing.

Then, Elijah called the people together. He built an altar and placed the sacrifice on it. He prayed to God to answer by fire. "Then the fire of the LORD fell and burned up the sacrifice, the wood, the stones, and the soil, and also licked up the water in the trench."[2] God demolished the entire altar with an instant flash of lightning.

At this point, Elijah and his people gathered the 950 prophets and executed them. Following the mass execution, Elijah ran back to the palace. In fact, he outran all the king's horses. But when he arrived, he found that Queen Jezebel was furious because of what happened at Mount Carmel and had ordered him executed just as her prophets had been. Elijah had just experienced a miraculous demonstration of God's power, but listen to how he responded to the queen's death sentence:

" . . . he arose and ran for his life . . . he himself went a day's journey into the wilderness, and came and sat down under a broom tree. And he prayed that he might die, and said, 'It is enough! Now, LORD, take my life, for I am no better than my fathers!'"[3]

What discouragement! What despair!

If God could demonstrate his power in such a mighty way, could he not also protect Elijah? So why was he so discouraged? First of all, he was probably exhausted after building an altar, calling down fire from heaven, killing 950 prophets and outrunning the king and his chariots. Secondly, he listened to the threats of a person, rather than trusting God.

When you are down and discouraged, cry out to God. Ask his Holy Spirit to encourage and empower you. God will always be faithful. **God...encourages those who are discouraged.**[4]

POINTS TO PONDER

1. Are you weary? If so, list some of the activities that may have contributed to this exhaustion, including seemingly "spiritual" pursuits.
2. Can you recall a time when you became down and discouraged simply because you were tired? Describe.
3. If applicable, list ways in which you might slow down from your busy lifestyle.

PRAYER

Father, like Elijah I am battle-worn, drained from daily activities, fatigued from fighting this fear. Allow me to rest in your presence, renewing my strength, reviving my faith. Let me not lose confidence in your mighty power.

[1] 1 Kings 18:24b, [2] 38, NIV
[3] 1 Kings 19:3-4, NKJV
[4] 2 Corinthians 7:6a, NLT

Notes:
_____
_____
_____
_____
_____
_____
_____
_____
_____
_____

THE BLAME GAME

The story of Job is a fascinating one. In his first wave of tribulations, four messengers came to his house while he was eating. The first told how enemies took his oxen and donkeys and executed the servants tending them. The second told of how lightning killed his sheep and more servants. The third told how the Chaldeans stole his camels and murdered still more of his servants. Then, the fourth messenger carried the worst news of all—a great storm killed all his sons and daughters.

What a tremendous tragedy! To lose all that you have in one day—one hour. The despair must have been overwhelming. Yet, here's how Job responded:

"Then he fell to the ground in worship."[1]

What? Even in the midst of all his troubles, Job worshipped God? Even when his friends mocked him for it, Job worshipped God? And the Bible goes on to say that "in all this, Job did not sin by blaming God."[2] Personally, I think I would have blamed God. After all, he could have stopped it. He allowed it to happen.

I have never directly blamed God for my panic attacks, but I have said in my heart, "Lord, you have the power to take these away, but you haven't." I blamed him indirectly.

How can I worship God in the midst of these attacks? I would wonder. They are too devastating, too debilitating, too much for me to handle.

Then I look at Job.

52

POINTS TO PONDER

1. Take a deep look into your heart. Who do you blame for your panic attacks?
   - Do you blame yourself? If so, why? Because God didn't make your mind strong enough to deal with these attacks?
   - Do you blame your family? Maybe your mother or father? Do you indirectly blame God for allowing you to be born into that family?
2. Looking back, have you ever blamed God directly or indirectly?
3. Is there anyone whom you have blamed for your condition that you need to forgive or to whom you need to be reconciled? Do you harbor any unresolved anger or bitterness toward that person that should be confessed?

PRAYER

Father, I know you have a plan for my life. I am sorry if I have ever blamed you for the fearful, fleshly condition of my mind. Show me the areas of my life that need healing. Reveal to me anyone I need to forgive or release. You are the God of restoration—you alone can cleanse and heal. Begin restoring me today.

[1] Job 1:20b, NIV
[2] Job 1:22, NLT

Notes:

_____

_____
_____
_____
_____
_____
_____
_____
_____

AFFLICTION

I don't believe God sends the fear and torment of anxiety and panic. However, God does allow the fear to come into our lives. If he is such a loving God, why would he allow this to happen? Maybe in our own sin and rebellion, the fear is a consequence of our thoughts and actions. Or maybe God uses these fearful situations to draw us closer to him. Maybe the fear can even save our souls or teach us about the commandments of God. Here is what King David wrote about his affliction:

"Before I was afflicted I went astray, but now I obey your word... It was good for me to be afflicted so that I might learn your decrees."[1]

It was good? How can affliction be good? How can panic attacks be good? This is a difficult question I have asked myself for years. I don't know the answer, but I have learned this: were it not for the fear that once controlled by life, I would not be a Christian today.

Before my "affliction" of panic disorder, I was a worldly man, caught up in the self-motivated goals of money and pleasure. When the panic struck, I first sought relief through the ways of the world: alcohol and indulgence. These failed to lead to peace, so I sought medical help. Tranquilizers and sleeping pills only yielded more temporary solutions.

The affliction grew. The bondage increased. The fear brought me so low that the only place to look was up. Doctors failed me; the world failed me; my family and friends failed me. I had no one left to trust but God himself.

I want to be careful when I make this claim that being afflicted is good because I have seen people's lives virtually destroyed by panic disorder. But we know that all things work together for good to those who love God, to those who are called according to his purpose.[2]

As odd as it may sound, I will be eternally grateful for the panic attacks that drew me to God.

POINTS TO PONDER

1. Have you grown closer to God or further away in your search for peace? Why do you think that is?
2. Make a list of "good" experiences in your life that resulted from affliction? If you can't think of any, ask God to reveal some to you.
3. Write down at least one reason you are thankful for your struggle with anxiety.

PRAYER

Father, I do not fully understand why you have allowed this fear to enter my life; however, I trust that you have a plan for my good. Reveal to me the good that you have brought into my life, and allow me to develop a heart of gratitude even amid affliction.

[1] Psalm 119:67, 71, NIV
[2] Romans 8:28, paraphrased

Notes:
_____
_____
_____
_____
_____
_____
_____
_____
_____

FAITH BUILDER

Going through my ritual review of emails early one morning, I came across this comment from a gentleman: "I can think of no bigger faith builder than panic disorder. If that is indeed the case, that our faith is being strengthened by this condition, then it is the biggest blessing we could ask for from God."

I must admit, this is not a comfortable statement. To declare panic attacks a "blessing from God" might seem ludicrous at first. Yet, I must grudgingly confess that my faith is stronger now than it has ever been.

Why? My faith has grown because I am learning to trust God totally, with all my heart, in every area of my life. I am growing to trust him more and more each day. When the fear begins to rise up within me, I could pour energy into fighting it, but I've lost that battle too many times. I am learning to trust God and rest during that adrenaline rush. To do that takes faith—faith that God will hold me and keep me safe no matter what happens.

One night I lay in bed, struggling with these mental intrusions. I was so tired, yet my mind was racing. I could feel the fear welling up within me. Next to me, my wife prayed. She knew.

As I lay there ready to leap out of bed, I thought to myself, *I could run and give into the fear. Or, I could stay here and trust God.* My body buzzed with adrenaline. My legs and arms tingled with fear. Running was the natural response. Yet, God's voice encouraged me to be still and trust.

Faintly, I prayed, "Lord, help me. Help me trust you more." The next thing I knew, the alarm went off in the morning. I awoke to a day filled with faith and confidence in my Father. He strengthened me and gave me peace, because I trusted him.

What we experience here on earth—no matter what it may be—should draw us closer to our Father. We must not focus on the problems and circumstances around us. Rather, we must look to our Father for strength and courage.

"For our light and momentary troubles are achieving for us an eternal glory that far outweighs them all. So we fix our eyes not on what is seen, but on what is unseen. For what is seen is temporary, but what is unseen is eternal."[1]

POINTS TO PONDER

1. Is your struggle with panic a "faith builder"?
2. Are you being drawn closer to God through your tribulations and troubles?
3. Does it comfort you to think that your troubles are only temporary? That you will be rewarded in heaven for your suffering?

PRAYER

Father, it seems that I have struggled with panic disorder for so long; and yet, I know that it will seem like a tiny blister in the light of eternity. If my fear has brought me closer to you, then I will count it a blessing—and not only anxiety, but any trial which works to build my faith and store up lasting treasures in heaven.

[1] 2 Corinthians 4:17-18, NIV

Notes: _____

_____

_____

_____

_____

_____

_____

_____

_____

_____

LEARNING TO CATCH

W e also rejoice in our sufferings, because we know that suffering produces perseverance; per-severance, character; and character, hope. And hope does not disappoint us, because God has poured out his love into our hearts by the Holy Spirit, whom he has given us."[1]

Rejoice in suffering? Using the words "rejoice" and "suffering" in the same sentence seems like an oxymoron. How can anyone tell me to rejoice in my sufferings? I am sure they never knew the fear, the terror, the bondage of panic attacks.

Why do we suffer? Why do we go through struggles and disappointments in life? Why do we have to learn to "deal" with problems like agoraphobia and life-restricting fears?

I wish I had all those answers. But, I don't. I can, however, share what the Word of God says. Our Father tells us that suffering produces perseverance—the supernatural ability to endure, the courage to stand firm and see the hand of God. Perseverance comes through being tested and challenged continuously.

When my son was two years old, I wanted to teach him to catch a ball. Since the motor skills and coordination of a two-year old are not fully developed, this proved to be a challenge. Each day, I would toss the ball up and he would throw his hands around like he was trying to catch it. His consistent dropping of the ball was occasionally interrupted by a successful catch.

"Yeah!" we all shouted. He kept trying. He persevered. In a matter of weeks, he was able to catch the ball more consistently. His perseverance resulted in the joy of success.

In the same way, we are faced with challenges every day. These challenges, as many of you can relate, are challenges that most people may not have to face. Going to the mall, driving a car, going some place by yourself or even going to bed at night can be colossal challenges for anyone battling panic disorder.

Yet, each challenge provides us with . . .

> . . . an opportunity to grow,
> . . . an occasion to learn, and
> . . . an option to persevere.

When we learn to persevere through our sufferings, we develop a more Godly character—a character which enables us to trust God through any circumstance. That Godly character births hope—hope that no matter what comes our way, God can be trusted.

Whenever you face a challenge, instead of asking God to remove the obstacle, ask him for the strength to persevere. Let him develop in you character and hope. You will learn to catch that ball. Soon, you will be so good at catching that you'll be able to handle anything that is thrown your way.

POINTS TO PONDER

1. What challenges do you face on a daily basis?
2. Do you find it difficult to rejoice over these challenges?
3. For each of the items you listed above, give one reason why you are thankful for that particular difficulty.

PRAYER

Father, thank you for my sufferings past, present and future because I know that through them I will become more like your Son. Give me the strength to persevere and the hope to rejoice no matter what my situation may be.

[1] Romans 5:3b-5, NIV

Notes:
_____
_____
_____
_____
_____
_____
_____
_____
_____
_____

CALLING THE BLUFF

I have learned that panic attacks are really powerful bluffs. They can actually trick your mind into thinking there is a serious, physical problem. Your body responds with a rapid heartbeat, increased blood pressure, tingling hands and a churning stomach.

All of these physical responses are real. The adrenaline released in your body is real. Everything about a panic attack is real except one thing—the source. Let me give you an example.

Imagine walking through a thick wilderness. As you approach a small river, you notice a large black bear feeding. At this point the bear hasn't noticed you, but your body begins to react. Your heart starts beating faster. Your blood pressure elevates. Your hands and legs begin to tingle as blood is being pumped to your legs for running and to your arms for fighting. Your stomach churns because your body is starting to digest food faster for extra energy. Adrenaline is being pumped into your body. During all this, your mind is focused on that bear, rather than on your body. If the bear sees you, then you are ready to react.

Someone having a panic attack will experience the same symptoms. Irrational fears arise because the person having the attack is "looking for the bear." Since no external danger can be found, the panic sufferer begins to listen to what their body is telling them. "My heart is racing. Maybe it's a heart attack." "My body is going numb. I must be dying."

In a panic attack, your body and mind responds to an unseen fear. If that's the case, then why can't we respond by faith to an unseen God? It seems like we have more "faith" in those unseen terrors that seek to destroy us than in our unseen Father who longs to save us.

Faith is the key to trusting God.

"Without faith it is impossible to please God, because anyone who comes to him must believe that he exists and that he rewards those who earnestly seek him."[1]

He may reward you with a new peace, a new courage, a new faith. Maybe it's a new hobby, a new accomplishment or a new day. Maybe he will reward you with a new job, a new joy or a new look on life. Maybe he will guide you to a new doctor with a new medication and a new task for overcoming these fears. God's blessings can be unlimited.

Call upon God today, and seek him. When you earnestly seek him, he will reward you. Talk to him in the mornings. Talk to him in the evenings. Call upon him by faith, and he will answer you.

POINTS TO PONDER

1. When panic hits, can you recognize that no real danger really exists? Are you able to remind yourself that the fear is conning you?
2. Does it seem that you spend a significant amount of time and energy seeking worldly solutions to your fears?
3. Do you believe God will reward you if you earnestly seek him? If not, why?

PRAYER

Father, I know that panic attacks are just a bluff, and yet they feel so real. Help me to respond to unseen faith rather than unseen fear, for I know that my faith pleases you.

[1] Hebrews 11:6, NIV

Notes:

_____

_____

_____

_____

_____

_____

_____

_____

_____

_____

GOD'S PLANS

There are times when I get so down and discouraged. I cry out, "Why, Oh Lord?" My heart feels broken with disappointment, pierced with hopelessness like a fiery arrow from the enemy. I pour out my heart to God as David did:

> **"But to You I have cried out, O LORD,**
> **And in the morning my prayer comes before You.**
> **LORD, why do You cast off my soul?**
> **Why do You hide Your face from me?**
> **I have been afflicted and ready to die from my youth;**
> **I suffer Your terrors;**
> **I am distraught.**
> **Your fierce wrath has gone over me;**
> **Your terrors have cut me off.**
> **They came around me all day long like water;**
> **They engulfed me altogether."**[1]

Yet, in the depths of my despair, God answers:

"For I know the thoughts that I think toward you, says the LORD, thoughts of peace and not of evil, to give you a future and a hope. Then you will call upon Me and go and pray to Me, and I will listen to you. And you will seek Me and find Me, when you search for Me with all your heart. I will be found by you, says the LORD, and I will bring you back from your captivity; I will gather you from all the nations and from all the places where I have driven you, says the LORD, and I will bring you to the place from which I cause you to be carried away captive."[2]

Be encouraged that God's thoughts towards you are thoughts of peace and hope. He does not send terrors to torment you. In fact, he wants to set you free from anything that binds you and hinders you from experiencing the fullness of life. He desires to give you hope, not despair, and a future where you can walk in peace.

POINTS TO PONDER

1. What would you like to tell God about your own doubts and fears? (Be honest. We can approach our Lord, as David did, without fear of punishment or judgment.) Do you feel imprisoned by these feelings?
2. Do you ever ask, "Why me, Lord?" Do you feel as if you are being punished?
3. What do you believe to be God's thoughts toward you? Write them down. What does the Bible say about God's thoughts concerning you?

PRAYER

Father, you know my every thought and fear, and still you love me. You say that your thoughts toward me are thoughts of peace, not of evil. You say that you desire to give me a good future, full of hope. Show me the good you have in store for me.

[1] Psalm 88:13-17, NKJV
[2] Jeremiah 29:11-14, NKJV

Notes:
_____
_____
_____
_____
_____
_____
_____
_____
_____
_____

THE SPIRIT OF FEAR

For God has not given us the spirit of fear, but of power and
of love and of a sound mind."[1]
This verse is often quoted when we talk to others about fear. It's
prayed over us when we humbly confess our anxieties. Yes, there's
hope when God talks about love, power and a sound mind. But I must
confess, I did not like this scripture.

Here's why?

When I did eventually let my guard down and share my
"condition" with other Christians, their canned response would
inevitably be: "But God hasn't given you a spirit of fear." Their eyes
would squint and their head would tilt as they stared at me with
confused looks on their faces.

Even though they didn't say it, here's what I heard, "You're a
Christian, but apparently you're not walking with God. What have you
done wrong?"

I know they meant well, but most people just don't understand
this condition. How could they? They have never experienced the
terror and torment.

So, for a long time, whenever I heard that scripture quoted, my
skin would crawl. I would play back those piercing, painful words and
looks from people. Even with God, I would cry out, "Well if you
haven't given me a spirit of fear, then why do I feel so afraid?"

It wasn't until a couple of years ago that I began to understand
this verse. A pastor said to me, "Russ, God hasn't given you this spirit
of fear. Yes, the enemy may have, but God hasn't. God wants you to
have love and power and a sound mind. That's his desire for you."

It's true. God has good plans for you.[2] Those plans do not
include fear, torment or bondage. Your Father's plans are peace, power
and purpose.

He has not given you a spirit of fear—a spirit that binds you
and holds you back. He has given you his Holy Spirit—the Spirit of
comfort and counsel. The Spirit of peace, power and purpose.

POINTS TO PONDER

1. Do you believe your "spirit of fear" comes from God or from Satan?
2. What does a "sound mind" mean to you?
3. How can you use the "sound mind" God has given you to battle the "spirit of fear"?

PRAYER

Father, thank you that you understand me even when others don't. I believe that you want what is best for me—power and love and a sound mind. I claim these gifts and resist every "spirit of fear" by the power of your Holy Spirit.

[1] 2 Timothy 1:7, NKJV
[2] Jeremiah 29:11, paraphrased

Notes: _____
_____
_____
_____
_____
_____
_____
_____
_____
_____

Fly Away

How many times have you just wanted to escape to some place where there is no fear? A place where you can rest and be at peace?

David longed for a place like that.

"My heart is in anguish within me; the terrors of death assail me.

Fear and trembling have beset me; horror has overwhelmed me.

I said, 'Oh, that I had the wings of a dove! I would fly away and be at rest—I would flee far away and stay in the desert. I would hurry to my place of shelter, far from the tempest and storm.'"[1]

Many times, I get so weary from struggling, fighting, wrestling with this fear. My mind becomes zapped of all mental energy. "Brain overload," I call it. Add to that the stresses of work, all the activities to which I so willingly say "yes" and the nameless other distractions. All of it adds up to a desire to fly away and be free.

"Oh that I had the wings of a dove—I would fly far away from the fax machines, the deadlines, the telemarketing phone calls during dinner, the congestion of 5 o'clock traffic. I would fly away to a place of solitude and rest. A place where the fear cannot find me—a shelter in the shadow of the Almighty."

Jesus told us of a place where we can go: "When you pray, go into your room, close the door and pray to your Father, who is unseen."[2]

Fly away to that secret place and shut the door. Escape for a few minutes from the cares of the world. Open your heart to God, and plunge right into his presence. When you are in his presence, fear cannot touch you.

Enjoy this place of refuge, this place of safety. Enjoy God.

POINTS TO PONDER

1. Do you ever feel as David did? Write down those feelings in your own words.
2. Describe the place to which you would like to "fly away."
3. Do you have a "prayer closet"? A place where you can shut the door and be alone with God? It may be an actual closet, your bathroom, your bedroom, your patio. Describe your special place. If you do not have a specific place, consider selecting one. If possible, go to that place now.

PRAYER

Father, I commit this place to you as my room of refuge, my solace from the storm. I long to fly away from the anxieties of this world, and so I come to you. As I commune with you, grant me a reprieve from the distractions of my life, the problems and the pain. Shelter me in your shadow.

[1] Psalm 55:4-8, NIV
[2] Matthew 6:6a, NIV

Notes: _____

_____
_____
_____
_____
_____
_____
_____
_____
_____

A PLACE OF REST

My shirt was drenched with sweat. It was supposed to be a friendly, Saturday morning get-together with some people from church, but this three-on-three basketball game was rough. I didn't know all of the best players would show up.

We only played about an hour and a half, but it was still an hour and a half too long for my weary body. The bumps, jolts, slaps and body slams took their toll on me physically. I needed rest.

When we finished playing, I glanced around quickly for a place to sit. The bench looked so inviting. As I sat down, my legs quivering, I sighed deeply. Ahh!

Rest is such a wonderful thing. Rest from a rugged game of basketball. Rest from a long day at work. Rest from a hectic schedule of activities and commitments.

What about rest for your soul? Rest from the intrusive thoughts and fiery darts of the enemy? Rest from the tug of war between fear and faith?

When you wrestle with fearful thoughts, your mind grows weary. Your emotions are tossed about like a rowboat in a raging storm. Is there rest? Is there peace?

"My soul finds rest in God alone; my salvation comes from him."[1]

There is a secret place where your soul can find rest. It's not a physical place—it's a place where your Father waits for you. A place where God will wrap his arms around you and hold you close. It's a supernatural place.

In this place, there is an indescribable peace. A peace that no matter what happens, God is there with you with his arms embraced tightly around you.

Trust is the key that opens the door to the secret place—to the quiet place where your soul can find rest. Open up your heart for God's loving embrace. He will keep you from harm, as long as you trust him.

68

POINTS TO PONDER

1. In what ways do you need rest?
2. Do you honestly believe there is such a place of rest? Do you trust God to meet you there?
3. Have you ever experienced a place of rest like this? If so, describe your experience? If not, what do you think would help you get there?

PRAYER

Father, my body, mind and soul are exhausted from daily battles. I have tried to find rest on my own, and yet I still feel drained. Help me to trust you more, unlocking the door to my heart, so that you can take me to that secret place of rest.

[1] Psalm 62:1, NIV

Notes:
_____
_____
_____
_____
_____
_____
_____
_____
_____
_____

WHEN GOD SHOWS UP

If you've ever experienced the terror of a panic attack, then you've undoubtedly prayed a prayer of distress. It's a prayer that comes from the depths of a tormented soul. It's not a superficial prayer or just a mouthing of words—it's a cry of distress.

God considered King David a man after his own heart.[1] Yet even David cried out to God for help when he felt afraid. I can imagine him groaning and weeping in prayer.

"In my distress I called to the LORD; I cried to my God for help. From his temple he heard my voice; my cry came before him, into his ears."[2]

When David cried out to the Lord, something happened—something unseen. God not only heard David's prayers—he sprang into action:

"The earth trembled and quaked, and the foundations of the mountains shook; they trembled because he was angry. Smoke rose from his nostrils; consuming fire came from his mouth, burning coals blazed out of it. He parted the heavens and came down; dark clouds were under his feet. He mounted the cherubim and flew; he soared on the wings of the wind. He made darkness his covering, his canopy around him—the dark rain clouds of the sky. Out of the brightness of his presence clouds advanced, with hailstones and bolts of lightning. The LORD thundered from heaven; the voice of the Most High resounded. He shot his arrows and scattered the enemies, great bolts of lightning and routed them. The valleys of the sea were exposed and the foundations of the earth laid bare at your rebuke, O LORD, at the blast of breath from your nostrils.

He reached down from on high and took hold of me; he drew me out of deep waters. He rescued me from my powerful enemy, from my foes, who were too strong for me. They confronted me in the day of my disaster, but the LORD was my support. He brought me out into a spacious place; he rescued me because he delighted in me."[3]

The next time you are consumed with fear and cry out to God for help, know this: you may not see any immediate response to your prayers with the natural eye, but something supernatural has begun.

There is a whole other world beyond your senses that has been affected by your cry for help. God does not simply dispatch a couple of angels to help you. He acts. He responds. He comes to save you himself.

What an amazing thought to know God cares for you so much!

POINTS TO PONDER

1. Do you believe that God will help you when you call on him? Why or why not?
2. Describe a time when God has rescued you from your enemy.
3. How does it make you feel to know that God cares for you enough to respond as he did in Psalm 18:7-19?

PRAYER

Father, release your wrath on my foe of fear. Thank you that you come to my rescue when I call on you; and help me not to doubt your strength or power, even when I think you are slow to respond.

[1] Acts 13:22, paraphrased
[2] Psalms 18:6, [3] 7-19, NIV

Notes:
_____
_____
_____
_____
_____
_____
_____
_____
_____
_____

WALKING THROUGH

W hen I first became a Christian, the panic attacks continued. I couldn't understand why. I prayed and begged and cried out to God for freedom. Yet, they continued. I kept asking God to take away the fear—to take away the bondage of panic. But, they continued.

Then one day, I was thinking about the people from the Old Testament and their situations. I learned something quite intriguing. God does not simply take away our problems—he gives us the strength to overcome them. We do not walk away from our problems—we walk through them. Let me explain:

A great flood poured down upon the earth. God did not save Noah from the flood. He saved Noah *through* the flood. He gave Noah the resources to survive.

Daniel's friends would not bow down to the king, so they were thrown into the furnace. God did not save them from the fire. He saved them *through* the fire. In fact, one "like the son of God" walked through the fire with them.

As Moses and the children of Israel were fleeing the Egyptians, they encountered the Red Sea. It seemed as if they were trapped. God did not save them from the sea. He saved them *through* the sea.

When God steps in and provides a miraculous deliverance, he gets all the glory. No man can take credit for the deliverance. There have been many times that I have prayed for God to free me *from* panic disorder. Now, I understand that he walks with me *through* the panic disorder. Peace comes as the flood and fire of fear have no effect on me.

"When you pass through the waters, I will be with you; and when you pass through the rivers, they will not sweep over you. When you walk through the fire, you will not be burned; the flames will not set you ablaze."[1]

When you walk with God, you can walk through any obstacle that comes into your path. Whether it be fear, panic, pain, confusion or danger, God will protect you when you walk side-by-side with him.

72

POINTS TO PONDER

1. Have you ever asked God to save you *from* your anxiety?
2. What "flood" or "fire" are you facing in your life today?
3. Do you trust God to walk with you *through* your circumstances?

PRAYER

Father, I know that you have the power to heal, and yet I also understand that sometimes you choose not to heal your children but to give them the sustaining grace to walk through their difficult circumstances. I pray that as I walk beside you, you will protect me from the fire and flood of fear.

[1] Isaiah 43:2, NIV

Notes:

_____

_____

_____

_____

_____

_____

_____

_____

_____

_____

Into the Storm

During our evening service last night at church, there was a great time of worship and singing. I could feel the presence and peace of God. I prayed for God's strength and courage to face my fears. As I closed my eyes, I saw this mental picture—a small wooden boat fighting hard against a huge, powerful storm.

I begin to think about this dark and stormy scene, applying it to my own life. Here I was, a small boat, fighting hard against what seemed like an invincible storm—a storm of fear. As the huge waves came crashing in, the boat was barely visible. I felt just like that small boat—thrashed, thrown, tossed up and down by the waves of terror and turmoil.

But, there was something very interesting about this scene: the boat was headed directly into the storm, waves crashing against the bow. The boat wasn't being driven by the storm. Rather, it was driving directly into the storm.

Now, I have no naval or sea-faring skills, but I will share what I have learned. When a storm approaches, the best course of action for any watercraft is to steer directly into the oncoming storm. First of all, this provides the most stable course for the vessel. If the boat is sideways when the storm hits, the smallest of waves can easily topple the craft. Secondly, if the boat is being driven by the storm, rather than against it, then the storm experience will last much longer, because you are being carried by the storm (read Acts 27).

I believe this picture I "saw" last night was God's way of showing me that I must face my fears head on, that I must steer my life right into the storm. (Psychiatrists call this "Exposure Therapy", where you confront your fears directly.) It's not a pleasant experience. In fact, it takes a lot of courage. But I believe with all of my heart that God will be with me as I enter the storms of discouragement and doubt.

> **"The floods have lifted up, O LORD,**
> **The floods have lifted up their voice;**
> **The floods lift up their waves.**
> **The LORD on high is mightier**
> **Than the noise of many waters,**
> **Than the mighty waves of the sea".** [1]

We live in a stormy world, and those worldly waves will crash hard against you. You can seek out the most comfortable course, but the storms will continue to rage. You can't outrun them. It's only when you charge headstrong into the storm that you will get through the storm. And always remember God is bigger than the storm, and he promises to guide you and protect you if you will trust in him.

POINTS TO PONDER

1. What storms have you experienced in your life? Describe.
2. Do you feel like you are being driven by the storm, or are you driving into the storm? What do you feel is the best course?
3. List some practical ways you can turn your "boat" into the storm rather than away from the storm.

PRAYER

Father, storms can be very fearful. They are so strong, so powerful. I don't want to face these storms alone. Give me the strength and courage I need to turn my life directly into the storm so that I can pass through it quickly. Be with me in these storms.

[1] Psalms 93:3-4, NKJV

Notes: _____

_____
_____
_____
_____
_____
_____
_____
_____
_____

After the Storm

I love sunsets. A few days ago while returning home from a business trip, I was again overwhelmed at the beauty of a sunset. As the plane began its descent into the Dallas/Ft. Worth area, the sun had just set below the horizon. The bright, blue sky slowly transformed into a deep orange. The beauty of it brought me to tears as I began to ponder the wonder of God.

Staring through that small, oval window, I thought back to other sunsets I had seen in my life. A few of them, I can remember so vividly. As I recalled each of those memorable sunset experiences, I discovered an incredible similarity: the most beautiful sunsets always followed an intense storm.

One evening, during my senior year at college in Austin, a tornado ripped through the area touching down in various parts of the city. We sat in our living room watching the local news, tracking the storm's movements across the area. Amazingly, the brunt of the storm passed right over us. We could hear the powerful winds outside ripping through trees.

But, the storm passed quickly, and everyone jumped back into the daily grind of things. I, on the other hand, went outside to survey the damage. Tree limbs were broken. Leaves were scattered. The wrath of the winds became obvious.

As I stepped out into the street trying to track the tail-end of the storm, I gazed upon one of the most beautiful sunsets I had ever seen. I quickly ran in and told my friends, "Come look at this!" They were reluctant at first but eventually agreed. Standing there in the street, we stared in awe at the thick thunderheads that were painted purple and orange. It was beautiful!

Our lives are full of storms. Storms of panic and fear. Storms that destroy and discourage. And just like the storms in Texas, these storms of life blow in quickly, doing lots of damage. Other times, they linger creating havoc and chaos. We question "Why, Lord?" We stomp our feet and cry out to God for comfort. Too often, it seems, our answer is painful silence.

Staring at that sunset just a few days ago from the plane, I sensed the still, small voice of the Lord say, "Russ, storms will come.

76

It's inevitable. But, where the storms destroy, I can rebuild. I can create the most beautiful sunset from any storm that blows into your life."

You can make it through the storm with God's help. Trust in him, and remember that God **"causes everything to work together for the good of those who love him and are called according to his purpose for them."** [1]

POINTS TO PONDER

1. Do you feel like your life is a storm? Describe.
2. Do you think it is possible for God to take the storms of life and shape them into a beautiful sunset?
3. Make a list of some previous storm experiences where God painted a beautiful sunset.

PRAYER

Father, while in the storm, it is so hard to see the beauty that can come of it. It just seems too powerful, too overwhelming, too destructive. Give me a glimpse of the sunset you have in mind for this storm. Give me the courage and peace to trust you in this dark hour.

[1] Romans 8:28, NLT

Notes:

_____

_____

_____

_____

_____

_____

_____

_____

_____

_____

OVERCOMING STRENGTH

I **have told you these things, so that in me you may have peace. In this world you will have trouble. But take heart! I have overcome the world."**[1]

I've had panic attacks most of my life. So after becoming a Christian, I expected God to work an overnight miracle that would forever free me from this fear. I prayed. I read scripture upon scripture about fear. I even waited…though somewhat impatiently. Nothing happened.

One day, I experienced a life-changing realization: God does not come into our lives to take away all of our problems. Rather, he gives us strength to overcome them.

God does not call us to be escape artists. He calls us to be overcomers.

Let me encourage you to be an overcomer this week. Here's what Jesus promises to those who overcome:

- "He who overcomes will not be hurt at all by the second death."[2]
- "To him who overcomes, I will give some of the hidden manna. I will also give him a white stone with a new name written on it, known only to him who receives it."[3]
- "To him who overcomes and does my will to the end, I will give authority over the nations."[4]
- "He who overcomes will, like them, be dressed in white. I will never blot out his name from the book of life, but will acknowledge his name before my Father and his angels."[5]
- "To him who overcomes, I will give the right to sit with me on my throne, just as I overcame and sat down with my Father on his throne."[6]

POINTS TO PONDER

1. What is your definition of an overcomer?
2. List some areas in your life that you feel you've overcome.
3. What are some areas with which you need to ask God to help you?

PRAYER

Father, You have already overcome the world. I want to join you in that victory. I want to be an overcomer. I want to conquer the fear, the doubt, the anxiety that plagues my life. Strengthen me with confidence to trust in you whenever I face trials. Show me how to rest in the peace that comes through the promise of eternal life with you.

[1] John 16:33, NIV
[2] Revelation 2:11b, [3] 17b, [4] 26, NIV
[5] Revelation 3:5, [6] 21, NIV

Notes: _____

_____
_____
_____
_____
_____
_____
_____
_____
_____

DINOSAUR DAY

It was dinosaur day at the local mall. The giant robots were so realistic. The mammoth models would move and growl like real dinosaurs. It was an exciting time for the kids.

Caleb was fascinated with dinosaurs, so we figured he would love to see the exhibit. As we walked into the mall, his eyes lit up when he saw the figures from afar.

As we came closer to the largest one, the T Rex, the growl grew louder and the eyes more fierce. Caleb was filled with excitement...and fear. His voice quivered when he pointed to the giant that hovered over us.

I tried reassuring him that it was only a model and that dinosaurs don't live anymore, but he was still consumed with the lifelike figures.

"Caleb? Hold my hand and I will help you. There's no need to be afraid." As we walked through the mall, his hand gripping mine, he began to enjoy the displays.

"Daddy! Daddy! Look at that one!" he shouted with excitement. "Over there! Look over there!" From fear to excitement, Caleb enjoyed the exhibit. Most of the time, he held firmly to my hand. Other times he gripped tightly around my neck.

He felt secure. He felt safe. His fear turned to joy when he walked with his father.

"For I am the LORD, your God, who takes hold of your right hand and says to you, Do not fear; I will help you."[1]

From a dinosaur model to the realities of life, fear takes on many forms. Although the reasons for the fear, in many cases, may only be perceived, our response is very real.

Let me encourage you to take hold of your Father's hand. Heed his words, "Do not fear." When you take your Father's hand and start walking, what once seemed fearful will become exciting. You can walk past the "dinosaurs" of life with a new confidence, a new peace, a new perspective, holding your Father's hand.

POINTS TO PONDER

1. List some of the "dinosaurs" in your life?
2. How do you feel when you encounter the threats you listed above?
3. Have you tried holding your Father's hand? If so, do these threats become less fearful when you do?

PRAYER

Father, take my hand in yours and lead me through the crises of life, turning my doubt into excitement, my fear into anticipation. Help me to trust you, hold on to you, in every situation.

[1] Isaiah 41:13, NIV

Notes:

_____

_____
_____
_____
_____
_____
_____
_____
_____
_____
_____

RUNNING TO MY FATHER

As kids, my brother and I shared a room. He slept on the top bunk, while I slept on the bottom. Going to bed at nights always presented a struggle for me. I can remember that bedroom so clearly. I would lie there pondering the inevitable—concepts like eternity and death. I didn't really know much about God, but those intrusive thoughts of "forever" terrified me.

One of my biggest fears as a child was the fear of death. To me, death meant staring at the lid of a casket unable to move for all eternity—not a pleasant thought. As my mind flooded with these unwanted thoughts, my heart would begin to race. I couldn't catch my breath. Numbness engulfed my body. Terror gripped my mind. I would pounce out of bed and run to my mom, screaming with a full-blown panic attack.

Nights like these were common. Oh, how I hated nighttime. I knew I had to win this battle with uninvited thoughts if I wanted any sleep. My mom always represented a place of safety. She was my refuge. She could calm the fears. I don't think she ever fully understood these episodes, but she was always there.

Today, I am learning how to run to my Father instead. I know that he can quiet my soul with tender "I love you's." I have found a new refuge, a sanctuary of security.

"Trust in Him at all times, you people;
Pour out your heart before Him;
God is a refuge for us."[1]

God offers a safe haven for each of us—a place where we can sit and rest in his presence. It's a secret place. Only you and your Father know about it. When you go there, your Father is already waiting for you. You can pour out your heart to him and tell him all that is on your mind. Tell him your fears, your doubts. You will hear his gentle voice say, "It's okay, child. There's no need to fear. I will protect you."

POINTS TO PONDER

1. Do you think about death often? Does it frighten you?
2. Do you have a refuge to which you run when fear assaults you? It may be a person, a place or a compulsive behavior. Describe this refuge. Does it remove your fear or simply replace it for a while?
3. Pour out your heart to God here on paper.

PRAYER

Father, you know my every thought, my every doubt and fear, and yet I try to hide my shortcomings by seeking shelter apart from you. I long to experience your peace. Teach me to run to you, my rock of refuge.

[1] Psalm 62:8, NKJV

Notes: _____

_____

_____

_____

_____

_____

_____

_____

_____

_____

LIFE AFTER DEATH

Jennifer's story reveals a fear similar to mine: "It all started when I witnessed a young boy (younger than me at the time, maybe three or four years old) get hit and killed by a speeding truck while he was riding his bike across the street. Thankfully, I do not remember the real gory details, but then I remember clearly the people and intense panic in the streets. I remember medical personnel and policemen everywhere. I was in sheer terror. My mother dragged me away quickly and got me away from the scene as quickly as she could. That was my first experience with death. I knew he was dead. I took it really hard and just was convinced that I was going to die soon. That was when the reality that we don't live forever hit. And just imagine: I was not even 5 years old yet. I was in for a long and scary life ahead of me."

At a tender, young age, Jennifer came to the realization that we don't live forever. Those inevitable questions immediately bombarded her—questions that we must all ask ourselves one day or another.

What will happen after I die? Is there life after death?

Three days after Jesus' death on the cross, several women went to anoint his body with precious oils. But when they arrived, an angel told them, "He is not here; he has risen, just as he said."[1] Jesus rose from the dead. He visited his followers. He ate with them. He talked with them. He laughed. He breathed. He lived! Death no longer had any power over him. Jesus proved that there is life after death. Death is not the end, but a beginning.

"Death has been swallowed up in victory. Where, O death, is your victory? Where, O death, is your sting?"[2]

84

POINTS TO PONDER

1. Is your concept of death jaded by past experience? Some traumatic event when you were young? Describe.
2. Do you have questions about death and eternity? Write them here.
3. Do you believe that Jesus defeated death through the resurrection? Why or why not?

PRAYER

Father, I know that I have no reason to be afraid of death, and yet my human nature fears the unknown. Replace my panic with peace as you make real to me the truth that your Son has removed the sting of death once and for all.

[1] Matthew 28:6a, NIV
[2] 1 Corinthians 15:54b, 55, NIV

Notes: _____

_____
_____
_____
_____
_____
_____
_____
_____
_____

DYING TO OUR FEARS

After talking with panic sufferers over the years, I have learned that many people's panic attacks are rooted in the fear of death. It's unknown. It's out of our control.

Death is not an easy subject to deal with. For years, I buried it with alcohol and other worldly schemes. In fact, I buried this fear of death so deep in my mind that I felt I had somehow attained immortality...until the fear resurfaced in a panic attack.

To face my fears, I began reading what God had to say about death and eternity in the Bible. I read about heaven:

"Then I saw a new heaven and a new earth, for the first heaven and the first earth had passed away, and there was no longer any sea. I saw the Holy City, the New Jerusalem, coming down out of heaven from God, prepared as a bride beautifully dressed for her husband. And I heard a loud voice from the throne saying, 'Now the dwelling of God is with men, and he will live with them. They will be his people, and God himself will be with them and be their God. He will wipe every tear from their eyes. There will be no more death or mourning or crying or pain, for the old order of things has passed away.' He who was seated on the throne said, 'I am making everything new!' Then he said, 'Write this down, for these words are trustworthy and true.'"[1]

Death is just going home. A home of rest. A home of peace. A home where there is no more fear, no more pain. You see, God longs for us to come home.

"Precious in the sight of the LORD is the death of his saints."[2]

The death of God's children is precious to him. Precious! What a powerful word. To God, our homecoming is precious.

POINTS TO PONDER

1. Do you think your anxiety may be rooted in the fear of death? Explain.
2. Describe your mental picture of heaven.
3. Are you certain that when you die, you will go to heaven? If not, ask the Lord to save you from spiritual death as you pray the prayer below.

PRAYER

Father, I believe that you sent your only Son to die for my sins and that he rose again on the third day. I know that by simply believing this and accepting Jesus into my heart, I will live with you in heaven forever after my physical death. Remove the fear of death and replace it with a longing to meet you face to face.

[1] Revelation 21:1-5, NIV
[2] Psalms 116:15, NIV

Notes:

ENTRUSTING THEM TO GOD

Another common fear for me is the concern about my family's safety. When my wife goes somewhere—to the grocery store or to the mall—I worry about her and my son. That ugly cycle of "what if's" consumes my thoughts.

What if they are in an accident?
What if someone attacks them?
What if...
What if...

Someone shared with me the following scripture when I explained this cycle of worry over my family: " . . . I know whom I have believed, and am convinced that he is able to guard what I have entrusted to him for that day."[1]

Even though most "what if's" are out of our ultimate control, we can find it so difficult to commit them to God. The key to victory over these fears is relinquishment. I am learning each day to entrust my family to God when those ugly "what if's" come crashing in. I know God is able to protect them. He is big enough to watch over them.

There are still times when I am suddenly consumed with fear about them or their safety. So, I immediately pray for their protection and re-commit them to God. Peace soon follows. However, this is not a one-time fix. The scripture says, " . . . for that day." I must pray daily over them.

If you face fears like these over loved ones, entrust them to God daily. Each morning, ask God to watch over them and keep them safe. Pray for protection and peace. Commit them to his care. Then let God do his job.

POINTS TO PONDER

1. Do you struggle with thoughts like these about your loved ones? Describe.
2. Has the loss or injury of someone close to you contributed to this fear? Could you have prevented this situation? Do you blame God for allowing it to happen?
3. Do you believe that God is able to guard what you have entrusted to him for today?

PRAYER

Father, God of the Universe, I know that you have special plans for my family and for me.[2] Forgive me for trying to control my own life. I commit myself, my loved ones and our safety to you.

[1] 2 Timothy 1:12b, NIV
[2] Jeremiah 29:11, paraphrased

Notes: _____

_____

_____

_____

_____

_____

_____

_____

_____

_____

IS ANYTHING TOO HARD FOR THE LORD?

I remember talking with a friend about the panic and fear that has consumed my life for years. After a lengthy explanation of what it was like to live with this condition, my friend responded, "Russ, I believe there is hope. I believe you can be free from this."

Immediately, I put up a wall of defense. "You don't understand," I announced. "It's easy for you to say. You don't have this crippling anxiety. I've tried everything to get free from this." My frustration and anger began to rise. My mind began to race through all the failed attempts to break free. Nothing worked for me. It was just too difficult.

In chapter 32 of Jeremiah, the prophet informed Zedekiah, king of Judah, that God planned to hand Jerusalem over to her enemies, King Nebuchadnezzar and the Babylonians. No one wanted to hear these words of judgment, including the king who imprisoned Jeremiah for his prophecy. The idea of the bondage that lay ahead must have overwhelmed the ruler.[1]

Yet Jeremiah beseeched the Lord: **"You have made the heavens and the earth by Your great power and outstretched arm. There is nothing too hard for You."**[2]

Even in the depths of my discouragement and fear, I know that my situation is not too difficult for the Lord. He can help me in spite of myself. Even in the captivity of my despair, the Lord's hand is not too short to save.

In response to Jeremiah's earnest prayer, God promised, "Just as I have brought all this great calamity on this people, so I will bring on them all the good that I have promised them."[3]

Let me ask you a question that God asked Jeremiah and Abraham:

"Is anything too hard for the Lord?"[4]

Think about it. Answer carefully.

POINTS TO PONDER

1. Do you really believe that your condition is beyond help? Beyond God's help?
2. Your situation may be too hard by yourself, but is it too hard for God? Why or why not?
3. Write down some issues in your life that were "too hard," yet with God's help you managed to get through them.

PRAYER

Father, there is nothing beyond your ability. You can do anything because you are God. Help me to know that my condition is not too hard for you touch. Show me that freedom is feasible and peace is possible. Give me the courage to trust your strength.

[1] Jeremiah 32:17, paraphrased
[2] Jeremiah 32:17b, NKJV
[3] Jeremiah 32:42b NKJV
[4] Genesis 18:14a, NKJV, Jeremiah 32:27b NKJV

Notes:
_____
_____
_____
_____
_____
_____
_____
_____
_____
_____

A VAIN HOPE FOR DELIVERANCE

A horse is a vain hope for deliverance; despite all its great strength it cannot save."[1] When I first began my quest for freedom, I was seeing a counselor about this panic disorder. We went through the typical barrage of questions and answers for a few weeks. During one of our sessions, I explained to her how important it was for me to travel with my cell phone. When she asked why, I explained how I could immediately call someone "just in case."

She called that a "safety valve"—the mechanism, habit or routine that each sufferer uses to help deal with a panic situation. For me, all I had to do was call someone when those terrifying thoughts would strike. By calling a friend or relative, I was forced to get the situation under control.

That was my safety valve, my pressure valve I could turn when the tension got to be too much, or the situation seemed to spiral out of control. As my heart raced wildly with anxious thoughts, I would reach for my valve of deliverance.

However, God warns us that our earthly safety valves are a "vain hope for deliverance."

Can horses really save? Can cellular phones really bring peace? Horses stumble. Phone batteries run down. It does not matter how strong, how reliable, how trustworthy we think our safety valve is, only God can truly deliver us. He wants us to call on him as our first response, not our last resort.

POINTS TO PONDER

1. Make a list of some of your safety valves.
2. Do you really feel like you can trust God no matter what happens? Why or why not?
3. Describe some areas in your life where you have trusted God in the past. Then make a list of some areas in which you want to trust him more.

PRAYER

Father, I know that nothing in this world can save me. Yet, I realize that many times I have placed my trust in a safety valve. Please forgive me for not trusting you, and give me the strength to trust you more.

[1] Psalm 33:17, NIV

Notes:
_____
_____
_____
_____
_____
_____
_____
_____
_____
_____

LABORING IN VAIN

K nowing the crippling power of a panic attack, I can relate to the need for a diversion or safety net. A diversion is anything that distracts your mind from an attack. A safety net, or safety valve, is anything that you cling to during an attack. These are natural responses to the terror of panic.

My diversion used to be alcohol. I could numb the fears with a few beers. Though I thought the alcohol provided an escape, it was really more of an anesthetic. And my cell phone was my safety valve.

In both cases, I placed my hope and my trust in "things." If my cell phone battery failed, I would panic. When the beer wore off the next morning, I was jittery and nervous. These worldly diversions and safety nets provided a vain hope for peace.

Slowly, I began to realize that I needed something solid and steadfast to hold on to—something that would not wear off or run down, something that could weather the storm of fear and panic.

My ability to trust God began to grow. He became my refuge in time of trouble. I could run to him when the terror filled my mind. Eventually, I ran to him instead of a beer or cell phone. When I allowed God to build my refuge of rest, I knew nothing could tear it down.

When you build worldly refuges, you labor in vain. All energy and effort put forth in these diversions and safety nets will be wasted.

Let God build your house of hope.

"Unless the LORD builds the house, its builders labor in vain. Unless the LORD watches over the city, the watchmen stand guard in vain."[1]

POINTS TO PONDER

1. You already listed some of your safety nets, or safety valves. Now list some of your diversions and distractions.
2. Do these tactics provide true escape or are they a waste of energy, simply masking or numbing the problem? Explain.
3. Describe the "house of hope," the "refuge of rest" you would like the Lord to build for you.

PRAYER

Father, I have labored in vain, placing my energy and trust in a worldly refuge. Forgive me. Help me to cease my striving, to lay down my safety nets and diversions, placing all of my hope and trust in you alone.

[1] Psalm 127:1, NIV

Notes:

_____

_____

_____

_____

_____

_____

_____

_____

_____

_____

HEALING HOPE

H ope. It is the one prospect that keeps people moving forward.
It keeps…
    …the faint striving.
    …the downcast aspiring.
    …the broken-hearted pursuing.
    …the lost searching.

Hope motivates us to get up each morning. We hope in God. We hope in peace. We hope for better things to come.

"Hope deferred makes the heart sick."[1] If we have no hope, then what's the use? Why go on? This verse goes on to say that " . . . a longing fulfilled is a tree of life."[1]

What do you hope for?

I hope for peace. I hope to be free from everything that keeps me from growing in God. I hope to have a closer walk with him. I hope to regain those areas of my life in which I have missed out because of panic attacks. These are intangible desires, that's why they require faith. Each one of us who has hope, has faith.

"But those who hope in the Lord will renew their strength. They will soar on wings like eagles; they will run and not grow weary, they will walk and not be faint."[2]

Hope can strengthen. Hope can uplift. Hope can heal.

POINTS TO PONDER

1. Do you feel faint, downcast, broken-hearted or lost? Explain.
2. Describe a time when "hope deferred" made your heart sick.
3. What do you hope for? If you can list something, then you haven't lost hope.

PRAYER

Father, God of hope, fill me with joy and peace as I trust in you, so that I may overflow with hope by the power of the Holy Spirit.[3]

[1] Proverbs 13:12b, NIV
[2] Isaiah 40:31, NIV
[3] Romans 15:13, NIV

Notes:
_____
_____
_____
_____
_____
_____
_____
_____
_____
_____

RUNNING THE RACE

I like running. Actually, let me rephrase that: I like the benefits of running. I don't enjoy the actual act of running. It's tiring. My body aches. My knees throb. I sweat like a horse. There is really nothing fun about it, now that I think about it.

But, I do enjoy the benefits of running: increased endurance, stronger heart, better breathing, reduced stress, lower body weight. (Notice I didn't say "low" body weight.) Yes, the benefits are good, but the work is not fun.

When I think of what it takes to overcome panic attacks and crippling fear, I think of jogging:

- A lot of work is required.
- You have to push yourself.
- It takes endurance.
- You can't give up.
- There is a finishing line.

"Let us throw off everything that hinders and the sin that so easily entangles, and let us run with perseverance the race marked out for us."[1]

To run this race, you need to "throw off everything that hinders you." When it comes to jogging, I wouldn't go out there in a three-piece suit. I wear my jogging clothes and running shoes. In this race against fear, do you "clothe" yourself with mental hindrances like doubt and hopelessness, or physical hindrances like too much caffeine or poor eating habits?

Throw off everything that hinders you—even sin. According to the Bible, sin can entangle you when you run this race for peace. But, if you confess your sin, God is faithful and just to forgive you of your sin.[2] Don't let sin entangle you. With Jesus at your side, you can be free to run this race.

I believe with all of my heart that a finishing line of peace awaits everyone who runs this race. Not just in death, but also in this life. It will take some work. You will have to push yourself. You will need endurance. You can't give up. And most of all, you've got to focus on the Goal.

POINTS TO PONDER

1. Do you feel like you are running a race? Does it seem too long, too wearisome?
2. Describe a situation in which you were just too tired to keep on running.
3. What is your Goal? What do you think God's goal is for you?

PRAYER

Father, give me the strength and endurance I need to run this race. Encourage me with your promises and your presence. Strengthen me physically, emotionally, mentally and spiritually. Let's run this race together.

[1] Hebrews 12:1b, NIV
[2] 1 John 1:9, paraphrased

Notes: _____

_____
_____
_____
_____
_____
_____
_____
_____
_____

WALKING IN THE DARK

L ate one afternoon, my wife was reading her Bible. "Russ," she said, "I want to read you this scripture."

As she read it, I half-listened—not really paying attention. "Wait, go back and read that again," I prodded. Something caught my attention.

"Who among you fears the LORD and obeys the word of his servant? Let him who walks in the dark, who has no light, trust in the name of the LORD and rely on his God."[1]

As she read, each word pierced my heart. I knew what it was like to walk in darkness, as do many of you. How many times do you feel lost, alone, empty, directionless because of the darkness of fear that surrounds you? You feel like your candle is smoldering down to nothing, and there is no hope.

Here's how I heard the words of that scripture in my heart: "Are you walking around all alone, empty, reaching around in the darkness of your fear? Reach out for God and trust him. Rely on your God."

Then, as I was drifting off into the new found revelation of this scripture, my wife interrupted me, "Russ, listen to this next verse."

"But now, all you who light fires and provide yourselves with flaming torches, go, walk in the light of your fires and of the torches you have set ablaze. This is what you shall receive from my hand: You will lie down in torment."[2]

Wow! "Lie down in torment." I knew that torment, as well. How many times have I lit my own torch in the darkness of fear and panic? How many times have I tried to walk in the light of my own efforts and strength?

I encourage you to lay down the torches you have made for yourself. Lay down your efforts, and trust God. Let his Light illuminate your way. His Light is more revealing, more healing, more peaceful than any light we could ever create.

POINTS TO PONDER

1. Do you ever feel like you are walking in darkness?
2. What "torches," if any, have you lit in an effort to navigate through your fear? Have they caused you greater torment?
3. In what ways do your "torches" differ from the Light of the Lord? Are your "torches" temporary? Do they provide a false sense of security?

PRAYER

Father, reveal to me the difference between the torches I have lit on my own and the Light you provide. Lead me from the darkness of dread and doubt as I trust in you, that I may no longer suffer the torment of my own futile efforts.

[1] Isaiah 50:10, [2] 11, NIV

Notes:

_____

_____

_____

_____

_____

_____

_____

_____

_____

_____

WHERE IS YOUR HOPE?

For anyone who has ever experienced the bondage of fear and panic, an overwhelming sense of hopelessness usually accompanies this gripping affliction. Without hope, the future is very bleak.

Yet, Paul encourages us to, **"...be joyful in hope, patient in affliction, faithful in prayer."**[1]

The hope we have is not like any other hope in this world. Our hope comes from the Lord. "No one whose hope is in [God] will ever be put to shame..."[2]

Today, I ask you a hard question: where is your hope? I know most of you reading this hope to be free from fear and panic. But, where is that hope directed? Do you hope in a doctor and his wisdom? Do you hope some new medication will finally work? How about that new counselor? Do you hope in your own abilities to beat this thing?

Please don't get me wrong, God can work through doctors and medication and counselors, but if your entire hope is placed in these alone, you will fall short of the peace God has waiting for you.

Another command Paul gives is to be patient in affliction. This command, I must admit, is not a pleasant one. I have met many people who are now free from this debilitating disorder. Their freedom did not come overnight. It took time and patience, birthed out of prayer, faith and hope. Paul may not have known about panic attacks when he wrote this, but God did. Our Father calls us to be patient.

Finally, be faithful in prayer. Although we may not understand or comprehend the "why's" of our condition, we must persevere in prayer. In that quiet time with your Father, he will impart hope and strength, peace and confidence.

POINTS TO PONDER

1. Where is your hope? Does it bring you joy?
2. Do you find it difficult to remain patient in your affliction? Why or why not?
3. Do you pray daily that God will either heal you from your condition or give you the strength to overcome it? If so, what results have you seen? If not, commit yourself to do so.

PRAYER

Father, my only hope is you. Forgive me for placing my trust in worldly and temporal remedies. Give me patience as I hope and pray for the freedom only you can bring.

[1] Romans 12:12, NIV
[2] Psalm 25:3a, NIV

Notes:
_____
_____
_____
_____
_____
_____
_____
_____
_____

FIERY FURNACE FAITH

King Nebuchadnezzar built a large statue. It was ninety feet tall, nine feet wide and made of purest gold. The king then made the following decree: "As soon as you hear the sound of the horn, flute, zither, lyre, harp, pipes and all kinds of music, you must fall down and worship the image of gold that King Nebuchadnezzar has set up. Whoever does not fall down and worship will immediately be thrown into a blazing furnace."[1]

Shadrach, Meshach and Abednego served God. They would not bow to any image the king had created. The king was furious and demanded that these young boys come before him. As they stood before the king, he told them directly, "When you hear the music, bow down!"

It was the king's decree. It was the law. If they disobeyed, they were surely going to die. Listen carefully to their response:

"If we are thrown into the blazing furnace, the God we serve is able to save us from it, and he will rescue us from your hand, O king. But even if he does not, we want you to know, O king, that we will not serve your gods or worship the image of gold you have set up."[2]

Did you hear the faith of these young men? Minutes before their obvious execution, they declare, " . . . the God we serve is able to save us from it, and he will rescue us from your hand." They did not bow to the king's demand. They did not give in to fear. No matter what the consequences, they were going to trust God, even if it meant death.

Many times when fear strikes, we give in to the thoughts and lies that have plagued us for years. The prince of this world plays the music of fear in our minds. When we hear it, we simply bow down to the fear and allow it to control our lives.

I encourage you to declare that you will trust God no matter what the consequences. As God protected those three boys from the fire, so he will protect you. When you trust God with all your heart no matter what could happen, his peace will flood your soul.

POINTS TO PONDER

1. In what ways have you bowed down to fear, now or at any time in the past?
2. How do you feel when Satan replays the music of fear in your mind?
3. Are you willing to trust God no matter what happens? Why or why not?

PRAYER

Father, I call upon you in my weakness and ask you to give me strength and courage—strength to stand against the music of fear, courage not to bow down to the enemy. I declare that I will trust you no matter what the consequences.

[1] Daniel 3:5, 6, NIV
[2] Daniel 3:17, 18 NIV

Notes:

_____

_____

_____

_____

_____

_____

_____

_____

_____

_____

Breakthrough Prayer

Prayer.

It's our direct line to God.

Sometimes, however, I feel like my prayers just hit the ceiling and go no further. My pleas seem to be tossed about in the storm of doubt and despair. There are times when I wonder if God really does hear my prayers.

I ask. I beg. I plead. Yet so many times I hear nothing but painful silence. Have you experienced this?

Let me share a story about Daniel. Cyrus was the king of Persia. During this time, Daniel had seen a vision about a great war. He mourned because of this horrific revelation. For 3 weeks, he fasted and prayed. He chose not to eat any choice food or drink. On the 21st day of his fast, something strange happened:

"I looked up and there before me was a man dressed in linen, with a belt of the finest gold around his waist. His body was like chrysolite, his face like lightning, his eyes like flaming torches, his arms and legs like the gleam of burnished bronze, and his voice like the sound of a multitude."[1]

An angel of the Lord had appeared to Daniel. The young prophet trembled and shook at the sight of this heavenly being. What is more amazing is what the angel said:

"Do not be afraid, Daniel. Since the first day that you set your mind to gain understanding and to humble yourself before your God, your words were heard, and I have come in response to them."[2]

Did you catch that? "Since the first day . . ." Daniel's words were heard by God on the *first* day he started praying and seeking God, yet there was no response for 21 days. Why? Read the next verse:

"But the prince of the Persian kingdom resisted me twenty-one days. Then Michael, one of the chief princes, came to help me, because I was detained there with the king of Persia."[3]

There was a war going on—a spiritual war. Heavenly forces were fighting to answer Daniel's prayer. It wasn't that God took three weeks to answer. God heard him on the very first day, but the supernatural struggle in the unseen world was holding back Daniel's answer to prayer.

When you pray, remember the following:
1. When prayed with humility, your prayers are heard the *first* day you pray them.
2. Spiritual resistance is real.

We are in a heavenly battle. The enemy wants us crippled by anxiety and fear. Let me encourage you to "set your mind to gain understanding and to humble yourself before God." Then, be patient and steadfast in prayer, and your answer will be sent from heaven to earth.

POINTS TO PONDER

1. Do you ever wonder if God hears your prayers?
2. When you pray for something and your prayer isn't answered right away, do you give up or do you continue to pray as Daniel did?
3. Have you ever prayed for something for a long time before you saw the answer? If so, describe your experience.

PRAYER

Father, thank you that you hear my prayers. Remind me to "pray continually,"[4] never losing heart, patiently awaiting your perfect answer in your perfect time.

[1] Daniel 10:5-6, NIV
[2] Daniel 10:12, [3] 13, NIV
[4] 1 Thessalonians 5:17, NIV

Notes: _____
_____
_____
_____
_____
_____
_____
_____
_____

LIVING FAITH

T wo men stood at the foot of a bridge. "It looks sturdy," declared the younger man. "I am sure it will hold us when we cross. There should be no problem. Look at that reliable construction. Look at the width of those wood beams. I am sure it will be fine."

The other man just stood there quietly for a few seconds. Then he headed out across the bridge.

Let me ask you a question: which one had faith that the bridge was strong enough to hold him? Was it the one who professed it was sturdy or the one who walked across?

Faith is more than just believing. It is more than just confessing. Faith is putting into action what we believe. It's not just waiting around for God to come down and zap us. If we never act upon what we believe, then we are not expressing our faith. We can talk all day about God's strength and protection, but if we never act on it—if we never step out—our faith is dead.

"Suppose a brother or sister is without clothes and daily food. If one of you says to him, 'Go, I wish you well; keep warm and well fed,' but does nothing about his physical needs, what good is it? In the same way, faith by itself, if it is not accompanied by action, is dead."[1]

Many people "talk the talk," but fewer "walk the walk." When trials come, faith will be tested. My faith was tested a few years ago. I boldly declared my confidence in God. But, when trouble hit, my life crumbled. My faith proved to be nothing more than a vain declaration. I really didn't believe what I was saying.

Today, I am able to act upon my faith in God. When the fear comes crashing in, I respond by not running away from the fear. Instead I accept the fear and believe that God will protect me and keep me safe. I put my faith into action by consciously choosing to rest in that belief.

You may ask, "Where do I start? How can I believe God's promises? How can I express my faith?"

Begin by praying for faith—faith to respond to God's promises. Read the Bible to learn more about those promises and God's faithfulness. Unlike that bridge, God will not sway or break. Our Father is strong and steadfast. He is faithful. He will never fail you.

108

POINTS TO PONDER

1. What are some ways you have "acted out" your faith?
2. What are some ways you have professed your faith, but did not follow it up with actions?
3. Has your faith ever been tested? If so, what did you learn from those experiences?

PRAYER

Father, there may have been times that I have professed my faith in you only to fail you. I ask that you would give me the courage and strength to stand in faith—to trust you no matter what comes my way.

[1] James 2:15-17, NIV

Notes:

_____

_____
_____
_____
_____
_____
_____
_____
_____
_____

TRUE FAITH

People often write to me saying: "Russell, I wish I had the faith you had, because then I could beat this anxiety."

I wish I had the faith that everyone thinks I have. The truth is I still struggle with fear. Anxiety is a dark cloud that still lingers over my mind. Sleepless nights are common. Yes, this battle with fear is not quite over for me.

At times, people's perception of faith is inaccurate. They see faith as the ability to believe for something. "If I can just believe in God more, then surely I can beat this thing." Or maybe this sounds familiar, "I just don't feel like God is helping me. If only I had more faith."

Let me share what I believe faith really is. When fear strikes, everything in me goes into high gear. My mind starts racing. My heart starts pounding. My legs go numb. I can't catch my breath. I am ready to fight or run. This is a natural reaction to fear.

When that happens, I don't feel God's presence, nor do I feel his peace. My "faith" is gone, and it seems like God is not real. It is not easy to experience these terrifying thoughts. So how do I respond?

The Bible says that God will never leave me nor forsake me.[1] It also commands me to trust in the Lord with all my heart, and not lean on my own understanding.[2]

So even when everything in me screams Run! or Fight!, I choose not to respond to those cries of fear. Rather, I choose to trust God—even if nothing makes sense. I choose to respond to God.

Is it easy? No. It's the hardest thing I've ever done.

Is my faith strong? Sure doesn't feel like it.

Faith is not how strong you feel it is—faith is how you respond even when God doesn't seem real, or things don't seem to make sense. It's how you respond to what the Bible says rather than what your feelings say.

Even if you don't feel like your faith is strong, I encourage you to respond to God, rather than to fear. When those anxious thoughts come crashing in, don't lean on your own understanding. Instead, trust God. **"And the peace of God, which transcends all understanding, will guard your hearts and your minds in Christ Jesus."**[3]

110

POINTS TO PONDER

1. How would you define faith in light of this message? Is your definition still the same or has it changed?
2. Describe a situation in which your faith has been tested.
3. How did you respond when your faith was tested? How can you respond in the future when your faith is tested?

PRAYER

Father, help me to understand true faith. Show me how to trust you in the darkness, when my mind can't comprehend all that is happening to me. Show me how to reach up and grab hold of your hand as you guide me through this valley of fear and anxiety.

[1] Hebrews 13:5, paraphrased
[2] Proverbs 3:5, paraphrased
[3] Philippians 4:7, NIV

Notes:
_____
_____
_____
_____
_____
_____
_____
_____
_____
_____

FAITH VERSUS FEAR

Over the years, I've heard numerous people teach on faith versus fear? It goes something like this: "Faith and fear are opposites. When you have faith, there is no fear."

I can't even count the number of times I've heard this type of message. But, I'll be honest with you: I don't like they way faith and fear are being preached like that. When I listen to those kinds of messages, this is what my mind hears: "Russ, if you just had enough faith, then you wouldn't be going through all this panic and fear. If you could just muster up enough faith, then you could be free."

All of a sudden, the burden of peace was on me; it was on my ability to believe. That defeats the concept of 'rest' when I have to do all the work.

Looking through the Bible, I cannot find any direct references that faith and fear are opposites. Rather, this is what I found: **"There is no fear in love; but perfect love casts out fear, because fear involves torment. But he who fears has not been made perfect in love."** [1]

In this scripture, I do see two opposites: fear and love. The scripture does *not* say, "perfect faith casts out fear." No. Perfect love casts out fear.

There is something about the love of God that breaks down the walls of fear. In my quest for tranquility, I've learned about my Father in heaven who loves me so much and cares for me in ways I could never comprehend. Truly, perfect love casts out fear.

The faith you need to fight fear is the faith that God really loves you, and that he cares for you. How much does he love you? Let the following scripture speak to your heart: "For I am convinced that neither death nor life, neither angels nor demons, neither the present nor the future, nor any powers, neither height nor depth, nor anything else in all creation, will be able to separate us from the love of God that is in Christ Jesus our Lord."

There is nothing natural or supernatural than can separate you from the love of God in Christ. Nothing. But, you must receive it. If I give you a gift, it does you no good until you receive it. Today, receive the love of God in a new way—a way that you can be made perfect in his love.

POINTS TO PONDER

1. Have you ever heard one of these messages on "faith versus fear"? How did it make you feel?
2. Have you experienced God's perfect love? If not, what could you do to experience more of his love?
3. Write down some of the ways God can show you his love.

PRAYER

Father, I want to know your perfect love. Help me to receive your perfect love in Christ. Show my any misconceptions or false thinking patterns that I may have about your love. Open up my heart that I may experience your perfect love that casts out all fear.

[1] 1 John 4:18, NKJV
[2] Romans 8:38-39 NIV

Notes:

_____
_____
_____
_____
_____
_____
_____
_____
_____
_____

Love Worth Countin'

Driving down the road one day, I asked my son, "Caleb, how much do you love me?" He stretched out his hands as wide as he could and said, "Daddy, I love you with twenty loves!"

His childlike concept of love was obviously based on some quantitative value system. You know, five loves for a grilled cheese, seven loves for the family pet, three loves for a Hot Wheels car, and twenty loves for his daddy.

Needless to say, I was touched. Twenty loves! That's a lot. I smiled proudly as I drove down the road.

A few days later, we were talking again, and Caleb said, "Daddy, I love you with duncountinluvs."

"What?" I asked curiously.

"Daddy, I love you with done countin' loves."

"Thanks Caleb!" I said, still wondering what "done countin' loves" meant.

A few days later, it hit me. He loves me so much that he's done counting the loves. He can't count any higher. In other words, his love for me goes beyond counting. Again, my heart melted.

What a wonderful childlike definition of God's love for each of us. His love knows no bounds. You can't count God's love for you. It's higher than any number you may try to assign to it. It's greater than any love a person can give you. His love is unconditional, based on who you are, not what you can do.

I want you to know and experience God's love. His perfect love drives out all fear: fear of man, fear of death, fear of the future, fear of fear. Through Jesus, God's love can reach down from heaven and touch you. God doesn't love you with twenty loves or a thousand loves or even a trillion loves. God loves you beyond measure. He loves you with "done countin' loves."

"I lavish my love on those who love me and obey my commands, even for a thousand generations."[1]

Caleb stretched out his hands as wide as he could and said, "I love you this much!" In the same way, Jesus stretched out his hands as he was nailed on the cross and said, "I love you this much!"

POINTS TO PONDER

1. Have you ever tried to assign a value of God's love for you? Can you comprehend his infinite love?
2. Do you think it is possible for God to love you any less now than he did the day you were born? Why? Why not?
3. Take a moment and write down some words of love you think God would speak to you.

PRAYER

Father, help me to experience your unconditional love for me. Lavish your love upon me that I may know I belong to you.

[1] Exodus 20:6, NLT

Notes:
_____
_____
_____
_____
_____
_____
_____
_____
_____
_____

CONFIDENCE IN GOD

For years, I've talked with people about panic disorder. And, each day I talk with someone new, the diversity of this disorder becomes more apparent.

For some, they haven't left their homes in years. Others can't drive alone. Some people have only had one attack—yet they live their life in the wake of that one attack. Others have attacks daily. Some have recovered within days of their first attack. For some, it has been a life-long battle.

For those who have found freedom from this fear, their testimonies carry one common theme: trusting God. Despite the differences in their situations, when they share their battles and victories, their conclusions are the same: "No matter what happens, I will trust the Lord."

I, too, have experienced the peace that comes from trusting the Lord. My first step on the road to recovery came years ago while sitting in that recliner when an attack hit. For the first time, I just said, "Lord, no matter what happens, I will trust you. If I die, then I will trust you. If I go crazy, I will trust you. No matter what happens, I will trust you." As quickly as the frightening thoughts had come, they were gone. Peace flooded my soul.

For years, I had sought other avenues for peace, placing all of my trust in someone's method for coping or some counselor's suggestion on how to breathe properly. All of these techniques are well and good, but they provide no permanent peace.

"It is better to trust in the LORD than to put confidence in man."[1]

Is there peace from panic? Can you really just sit still while your mind and body explode with terror? I have. Others have. Peace comes from trusting in the Father.

116

POINTS TO PONDER

1. Describe your personal battle with panic and anxiety?
2. Where is your confidence? Is it in doctors and counselors or in the Great Physician?
3. Have you ever been able to say, "Lord, no matter what happens, I will trust you?" If so, describe the outcome. If not, do it now.

PRAYER

Father, I place my trust in you alone.

[1] Psalm 118:8, NKJV

Notes:

_____

_____

_____

_____

_____

_____

_____

_____

_____

_____

Swimming Lessons

Don't let your hearts be troubled. Trust in God, trust also in me."[1]
Reading through my Bible one day, I came across this scripture. It was as if Jesus were saying directly to me, "Russ, don't worry. Don't let your heart be troubled." And then he explained how: "Trust in God, and trust in me."

One summer, my wife and I enrolled our son in his first swimming lesson. He was only a year old. He couldn't walk. He could barely crawl. But after two weeks, he could hold his breath and swim. It was amazing! One thing, in particular, caught my attention—the way he trusted us. When we called him to come to us in the water, he swam knowing we would not let him sink. He showed no fear.

God wants us to trust him like that—like a child. We may feel at times as if we are sinking, headed right to the bottom. We panic. We splash. We kick. We gasp for air. Yet, in the midst of the chaos, our Father's hands are reaching out to rescue us.

Why does our Father take us into this pool of pain? Why does it sometimes feel like he is letting us sink?

I wanted my son to learn to swim so that he could enjoy the water instead of fear it.

Trials will come. Pain is unavoidable. But our Father will always be there with his arms reaching out to hold us. We can always trust that he will never let us drown.

POINTS TO PONDER

1. What "pools of pain" in your own life come to mind?
2. Have you ever felt like your heavenly Father would let you drown? If so, why?
3. Can you identify some of your spiritual swimming lessons? Describe them. What did you learn from those experiences?

PRAYER

Father, the pool of pain is not a pleasant place to be. Pain often points to a problem that needs attention and healing. Reveal to me the purpose of my pain. Help me to feel your arms uphold me in the waters of fear and doubt.

[1] John 14:1, NCV

Notes: _____
_____
_____
_____
_____
_____
_____
_____
_____
_____

ABANDONMENT

Can a mother forget the baby at her breast and have no compassion on the child she has borne? Though she may forget, I will not forget you! See, I have engraved you on the palms of my hands; your walls are ever before me."[1]

Can a mother really forget her baby? Today, you read of such shocking stories in the newspaper:

"Crying infant found in trash can..."

"Teenage mother abandons newborn..."

"Mother murders her child in a fit of rage..."

These kinds of stories break the heart of any reader. Abandonment. Desertion. Rejection. An innocent child destroyed or forsaken by a selfish mother.

God is not like that. He is a God of compassion. He declares, "Though she may forget, I will not forget you!" God will not abandon you or cast you aside. He will be with you no matter what you have done.

Not only that, your name is engraved in the palm of his hand. Can you imagine? There, engraved in the palm of God's hand is "Russell Lee Pond." And, so is your name.

Did you ever write things in the palm of your hand? Love notes, phone numbers, formulas for your math test? Sometimes they were notes of affection. Other times, they were reminders.

In the palm of God's hand is a reminder of his love towards you. It's not written in ink, which can rub off or smear. It is *engraved* in the palm of his hand. Everyday, he sees that reminder.

I can just picture God reading your name in his hand and pulling his arms up against his chest saying, "Oh, how I love this child of mine." I can imagine the emotion, the joy that fills your Father's heart when he thinks of you, his precious child.

When you feel abandoned or rejected, when you feel all alone, look at the palm of your hand. Remember that God has your name etched in his.

120

POINTS TO PONDER

1. Have you ever been rejected by family or friends in some way? Describe what happened and how it made you feel.
2. What is engraved in God's hand? Write it down.
3. How does it make you feel to know that God will never forget about you or abandon you?

PRAYER

Father, thank you that you will never leave me nor forsake me.² *As you have carved my name on your palm, write your name on my heart, that all who see me may know that I am your child.*

¹ Isaiah 49:15-16, NIV
² Hebrews 13:5b, paraphrased

Notes: _____
_____
_____
_____
_____
_____
_____
_____
_____
_____

HIS THOUGHTS TOWARDS US

If you are feeling like God has forsaken you or given up on you, then read these words from Psalm 139. Let them sink deep into your heart. God cares for you more than you can fathom. His love for you reaches through the Cross and embraces you.

"O LORD, you have examined my heart and know everything about me. You know when I sit down or stand up. You know my every thought when far away. You chart the path ahead of me and tell me where to stop and rest. Every moment you know where I am. You know what I am going to say even before I say it, LORD. You both precede and follow me. You place your hand of blessing on my head.

Such knowledge is too wonderful for me, too great for me to know! I can never escape from your spirit! I can never get away from your presence! If I go up to heaven, you are there; if I go down to the place of the dead, you are there. If I ride the wings of the morning, if I dwell by the farthest oceans, even there your hand will guide me, and your strength will support me. I could ask the darkness to hide me and the light around me to become night—but even in darkness I cannot hide from you. To you the night shines as bright as day. Darkness and light are both alike to you.

You made all the delicate, inner parts of my body and knit me together in my mother's womb. Thank you for making me so wonderfully complex! Your workmanship is marvelous--and how well I know it. You watched me as I was being formed in utter seclusion, as I was woven together in the dark of the womb. You saw me before I was born. Every day of my life was recorded in your book. Every moment was laid out before a single day had passed.

How precious are your thoughts about me, O God! They are innumerable! I can't even count them; they outnumber the grains of sand! And when I wake up in the morning, you are still with me!

Search me, O God, and know my heart; test me and know my thoughts. Point out anything in me that offends you, and lead me along the path of everlasting life."[1]

122

As a father, I love hugging my little boy. Even more, I love it when he hugs me, or as he calls it, "big squeezers." Just typing those words brings tears to my eyes. How much more does God enjoy it when we embrace him?

I don't think anyone can truly understand how much God thinks about one of his children. His thoughts outnumber the very grains of sand throughout the earth. That's a lot!

Today, spend some time and soak in the sweetness of his love.

POINTS TO PONDER

1. Do you find it difficult to believe that God can know you completely and still love you?
2. How have you tried to "run" from the Spirit of God? How does it make you feel to know that even when you try, you cannot escape God's presence?
3. Do you believe you are made in an "amazing and wonderful way"? Have you ever blamed God for your imperfections?

PRAYER

Father, you have made me perfectly according to your plan, and you love me despite my weaknesses. Forgive me for being dissatisfied with the way you have created me; and thank you that you will always be with me, thinking of me, loving me.

[1] Psalm 139:1-18, 23-24, NLT

Notes: _____

_____
_____
_____
_____
_____
_____
_____
_____
_____

HEARING GOD

As sheep, we have a Shepherd who guides us and leads us. Jesus said, **"My sheep listen to my voice; I know them, and they follow me."**[1]

God can "speak" many different ways. He can speak through the Bible. He can speak through prayer. He can speak through others. He can speak in visions or dreams. He can speak through our conscience.

But God is not the only voice speaking to us. The enemy has a voice. His voice can sound similar, but the words are not words of love—they are words of lies. Satan is a liar and the father of lies.[2]

God's voice leads and guides.

The enemy's voice pushes and condemns.

In his book *Hearing God*, Peter Lord talks about positive focusing and negative filtering. Positive focusing denotes listening for that one special voice we want to hear.[3] When our baby was born, we could be in a crowded room with a cacophony of noises, and my wife could hear the faint whimper of our boy. It was incredible! In the same way, we can develop a sensitivity for God's gentle voice.

Negative filtering allows us to filter out negative noises.[3] My wife and I lived underneath the flight pattern of the Dallas/Ft. Worth airport. Every 3 or 4 minutes, a jet would fly over. When we first moved there, it was quite annoying. However, in time, we were able to filter out those sounds. It was as if we didn't hear them any more. Now, did the planes get quieter? No. We just developed negative filtering.

In the same way, we must learn to focus on God's voice and filter out the voice of the enemy. By doing this, we will be led by love, by the very voice of God. Much of the fear and panic we feel is a result of the enemy's voice. He speaks lies, doubts, fears and "what if's" into our mind. We need to learn to filter those messages out and focus on God's voice: "I love you, my child. I will take care of you. I will hold you. Trust me."

POINTS TO PONDER

1. In what ways has God spoken to you in the past?
2. In what ways has the enemy spoken to you?
3. List some ways you can further develop your positive focusing and negative filtering.

PRAYER

Father, awake my spiritual ears to your voice. As I hear you, help me to follow you as sheep follow their shepherd, never deceived by the wolf who threatens to lead them astray and devour them.

[1] John 10:27, NIV
[2] John 8:44, paraphrased
[3] Lord, Peter. *Hearing God.* Baker Books, Grand Rapids, MI, 1988.

Notes: _____

_____
_____
_____
_____
_____
_____
_____
_____
_____

A FATHER'S EMBRACE

It had been a rough night. Fear and anxiety was like a strong coffee keeping me awake. I decided to lie down with my little boy. I find so much pleasure and peace in watching him sleep.

As I quietly crawled into bed, I pulled the covers over us and gently wrapped my arms around him.

He was so peaceful.

As I began to stroke his hair with one hand and embrace him with the other, a question came to mind: *Do you think Caleb has any idea you are there holding him, kissing him, protecting him, lavishing your love upon him?*

No.

Then, I felt the Lord speak to my heart: *Russ, the same is true for me. I am holding you, kissing you, protecting you, lavishing my love upon you; yet, you have no idea that I am here with you.*

As I wiped away the tears from my eyes, I felt a new sense of God's presence—not a tangible presence, but a presence that is accepted by faith.

God's arms of love were embracing me.

He was protecting me.

His gentle hand was caressing my head.

My Father was pouring out his love for me.

The next time you feel alone, abandoned, far away from God, know that he is not far away from you. He is closer than you realize. He is your hiding place. He will shelter you in his arms of love. He will sing songs over you. Songs of peace and freedom. Songs of deliverance.

"You are my hiding place; you will protect me from trouble and surround me with songs of deliverance."[1]

126

POINTS TO PONDER

1. Do you ever feel alone, abandoned, far away from God? Describe those feelings.
2. Do you feel that God is with you at this moment? Why or why not?
3. Write a "Song of Deliverance," words that you would like to hear the Lord sing to you.

PRAYER

Father, thank you that you are with me always,[2] even when I fail to recognize your presence. Make my spirit more sensitive, that I may feel your arms embracing me, protecting me. You are my hiding place.

[1] Psalm 32:7, NIV
[2] Matthew 28:20b, paraphrased

Notes: _____

_____

_____

_____

_____

_____

_____

_____

_____

THE APPLE OF HIS EYE

Driving home one day after work, I savored the words of an email I had received that morning: "Russ, I am impressed with you." Catering to my ego, I replayed those words over and over in my mind. It felt good to know that I had impressed someone.

My waves of pride were interrupted by a gentle, quiet voice, "Russ, I am impressed with you."

Curiously, I thought, *Why would God be impressed with me? I'm far from perfect. I've failed him many times before. No, that can't be God.* Yet, the thoughts continued. I couldn't get those words out of my head. "I am impressed with you."

I questioned God, "Why me? Why are you impressed with me? I haven't done anything worthy of your attention, let alone your accolades."

Then, I began to think about my son:

"Caleb's the best swimmer in his class."

"You know, he can already kick that soccer ball."

"For a two-year-old, he can speak so well."

Yes, I am impressed with my son.

I realized then that it's not what he does that impresses me—it's who he is. He is my child. I began to understand the gentle words of my Father. He is impressed with me for who I am, not for what I do. I am his child.

Think for a second how parents talk about their children. They constantly brag about their accomplishments, their achievements, their awards. No one can compare to their child. They are esteemed high above all other children.

Today, know that your Father is impressed with you. No matter what you have experienced or battled or overcome, God is impressed with you. You are his child, his joy, his prized possession. You are the apple of his eye, and he will care for you and keep you safe.

"He shielded him and cared for him; he guarded him as the apple of his eye."[1]

128

POINTS TO PONDER

1. Can you think of any reasons why God would be impressed with you?
2. Do you believe that God is proud of you whether you listed ten reasons to the previous question or zero?
3. How does it make you feel to know that you are the "apple" of God's eye?

PRAYER

Father, I have done nothing impressive in my life, nothing worthy of commendation or praise; and, yet, you esteem me as one of your own—a child of the King. Thank you for such unsurpassable grace and mercy.

[1] Deuteronomy 32:10b, NIV

Notes:
_____
_____
_____
_____
_____
_____
_____
_____
_____
_____

GOD REJOICES OVER YOU

The LORD your God is with you, he is mighty to save. He will take great delight in you, he will quiet you with his love, he will rejoice over you with singing."[1]
The first part of this scripture is very encouraging: "The Lord your God is with you, he is mighty to save." No matter where you are or how bad things look, God is with you. Not only is he with you, he is ready to save you when you call out to him.

However, it's the second part of the scripture that touches me most: "He will take great delight in you."

What? The Maker of the Universe delights in me? Oh, but I have done so much to cause him pain or grief. Surely, he can't delight in me. If only he knew my thoughts and the things I have done.

He does know. He has seen it all. Yet, if you have truly accepted Jesus Christ into your heart by faith, he still delights in you. The key is his Son Jesus. Because Jesus died as punishment for our sins, God does not see sinners when he looks at believers . . . he sees his children as saints.

Not only that, "He will rejoice over you with singing."

Can you imagine God—Almighty God—in heaven right now singing over you? Can you imagine him rejoicing over you with songs and dancing? God is rejoicing in heaven this very moment over you. It's not one big celebration for everyone. It's a single celebration just for you.

Why me? Why does he celebrate over me? I can't even get along with the neighbors, and God is rejoicing in heaven for me? Why me?

God rejoices because of his great love for you. He loves you more than you could ever imagine. When things look fearful and frightening, let his love quiet you. Let his love still your heart. If he is in heaven rejoicing over you, then surely he cares about how things are going for you down here.

Today, spend some time rejoicing with God. I am sure you can't out-dance or out-sing the Lord. But, wouldn't it be fun to try?

130

POINTS TO PONDER

1. Do you really feel in your heart that God takes great delight in you?
2. How does it make you feel to know that God is singing, dancing, rejoicing over you?
3. If you have a hard time believing that God wants to rejoice over you, then list a few reasons why.

PRAYER

Father, I may not fully understand how and why you rejoice over me, but I ask that you would help me to rejoice with you. I want to receive your love and your joy that you want to pour over me.

[1] Zephaniah 3:17, NIV

Notes:

_____

_____

_____

_____

_____

_____

_____

_____

_____

MOVED WITH COMPASSION

While teaching elementary school, my wife told me about a student she had been working with. He wasn't a serious troublemaker, but because of emotional battles at home, he continually faced disciplinary struggles at school.

One afternoon, my wife and I were at the movies. As we walked out of the theater, up runs this little boy and hugs my wife.

"Hi Mrs. Pond! Did you like that movie?" I watched as they chatted and swapped smiles.

As we climbed into the car, an overwhelming wave of compassion hit me. I wept and wept. I couldn't help it. I kept telling my wife, "It's not his fault. It's not his fault." It was as if God was allowing me to feel the emotional pain this little boy had experienced.

What I experienced that afternoon was just a taste of the compassion God has for each of us. He knows exactly what we are going through. He hurts when we hurt. It pains him to see us struggle. But, our Father doesn't just stop at compassion. He is moved to act upon that compassion by comforting you.

"Praise be to the God and Father of our Lord Jesus Christ, the Father of compassion and the God of all comfort, who comforts us in all our troubles, so that we can comfort those in any trouble with the comfort we ourselves have received from God."[1]

This scripture has become my mission statement in life: to comfort people with the comfort I myself have been comforted with.

When I saw that little boy, I wanted to find out how we could get more involved with his life. I wanted him to know that people love him and care about him. I was moved with the compassion to act.

God is moved by his compassion towards you. Do you hear your Father's heart? Do you hear him weeping with you? Do you hear him celebrating your victories with you? Ask him. You will hear that still, small voice say, "I am."

132

POINTS TO PONDER

1. Have you ever experienced a glimpse of God's compassion? If so, describe the experience.
2. List some people, organizations or ideas about which you feel compassionate.
3. Recall a time when you were so moved with compassion, that it provoked you to action.

PRAYER

Father, I know that you care so much for us, your children. Help me to see others through your eyes—eyes of compassion. Help me to get involved when possible to help those who are in need. I desire to be moved with compassion.

[1] 2 Corinthians 1:3-4, NIV

Notes:
_____
_____
_____
_____
_____
_____
_____
_____
_____
_____

GOING THROUGH THE MOTIONS

It was a cheap toy. I'm still not quite sure where we got it, but this little, lime-green spinning top was Caleb's favorite toy for the week.

Although he couldn't spin it, he played with it like any other toy. Every now and then, he'd ask us to spin it for him. He enjoyed watching it balance and spin almost miraculously on its tip. You could tell from the expression on his face that he really wanted to know how it worked. Even more, he wanted to learn to spin it himself one day.

Early one morning, Caleb came running into my office. "Daddy?" he asked expectantly. "Will you spin it for me?"

I stopped what I was doing and spun the cheap toy a few times. As before, his eyes were glued to the spinning object. Occasionally, he would turn to me, smile and giggle.

"I wanna spin it," said the curious two-year-old. I took his hand in mine and showed him how to snap our fingers. With my hand over his, I went through the motions of grasping the top's handle between the fingers.

Then, I sat back and watched him try.

He fumbled around with the top a few times. Then, with one smooth motion, he spun the top. I was surprised! He was surprised! We both started shouting, "Yeah!" It was an exciting time, to say the least.

For most, it may have been no big deal. For my son and me, it marked a special occasion. A time of teaching, a time of learning. Most of all, a time of rejoicing.

Life is very similar. We fumble around with so many "toys," unable to succeed because of inexperience or fear. Yet, our Father takes our hands and our heart and gently goes through the motions with us. He shows us how to do those tasks we keep telling ourselves we can't do. He shows us how to spin those tops.

"With man this is impossible, but with God all things are possible."[1]

But, God doesn't stop there. Just as my son and I shouted with excitement, your Father rejoices with you in your victories. His heart leaps with yours as you put into motion what he has taught you.

POINTS TO PONDER

1. Is there any activity that seems impossible to you right now? If so, what?
2. Can you recall any times in the past when you could feel God "going through the motions with you," helping you to accomplish a seemingly difficult task?
3. Have you ever sensed God rejoicing with you in your victories? If so, describe your feelings.

PRAYER

Father, my life seems almost impossible at times, and yet I know that with you all things are possible. Take my hands in your mighty hand, my heart in your loving heart, and show me how to meet the tasks that lie before me, so that we may rejoice together in the victory.

[1] Matthew 19:26b, NIV

Notes:
_____
_____
_____
_____
_____
_____
_____
_____
_____
_____

Head Start

Two weeks after graduating from college, I moved away from home to start my new career. I was young. I was excited. I was also very alone.

To add some life to my lonely days, I decided to buy a puppy. I've enjoyed dogs ever since I was a kid. I knew that having this new pet would help break the monotony of solitude.

Keesha was a playful puppy, and our favorite game was called "Find Harold." Harold was a small, stuffed teddy bear that she cherished.

To start the game, I covered Keesha's eyes and threw Harold across the room. Then I would release my hand from her eyes and shout, "Find Harold!" Her eyes would dart back and forth, then she would pounce around the room trying to find Harold.

Most of the time she was successful, but there were times when she just couldn't find him. She would run back to me with this pitiful "help me" look on her face. So, I would grab her head and set her in the direction of Harold. I held her head firm until I could feel her excitement as she spotted Harold. Then off she leapt to retrieve her treasured toy.

In many ways, I feel like God wants to hold our heads and set our hearts toward his kingdom—a kingdom full of peace and purpose. Excitement fills our hearts as we begin to see where we are to run. Then, in his timing, he releases us to run toward our calling and purpose.

"Do not set your heart on what you will eat or drink; do not worry about it. For the pagan world runs after such things, and your Father knows that you need them. But seek his kingdom, and these things will be given to you as well."[1]

Today, I encourage you to run to God. Let him lovingly take your head, your mind into his hands. Let him point you in the direction where you are to run. When you begin to see a future full of hope and peace, excitement will fill your heart.

POINTS TO PONDER

1. Do you sometimes feel you are darting here and there trying to find peace and purpose with little or no success?
2. Do you have a good idea of what you want in life (peace, joy, etc.) but can't seem to find it? Make a list of what you want.
3. Where is your heart set? Is it set on the things of this world, or on God's kingdom?

PRAYER

Father, I long to seek first your kingdom and your righteousness. Take my spirit in your loving hands and point me in the direction you would have me go. Then, when I am ready to run, release me to my calling that I may draw closer to you and experience all the blessings you have in store for me.

[1] Luke 12:29-31, NIV

Notes: _____

_____

_____

_____

_____

_____

_____

_____

_____

_____

FORMULAS

By trade, I'm an engineer. Much of engineering is based on the foundations of math, so plugging in formulas is a way of life for me.

Formulas are nothing more than expressions of facts. For example, look at this simple formula: $1 + 2 = 3$. It's a fact. No matter how many times you "run the math," one plus two will always equal three.

Formulas and mathematical expressions are consistent by all natural laws. Yet, when it comes to God, are there such things as spiritual formulas? Can I do A and B so that God can do C? I have heard it preached that "God is not a formula God."

Yet, there are some promises of God that are based on conditions. Like a formula or mathematical expression, these conditions will lead to a result. For example, if you fully obey the Lord, you will be blessed.[1] And, "... if you confess with your mouth, 'Jesus is Lord,' and believe in your heart that God raised him from the dead, you will be saved."[2]

Why do I bring all this up? Good question. I want to share a "formula" promise I found in the Psalms that relates to our health, both natural and mental.

"Oh, the joys of those who are kind to the poor. The LORD rescues them in times of trouble. The LORD protects them and keeps them alive. He gives them prosperity and rescues them from their enemies. The LORD nurses them when they are sick and eases their pain and discomfort."[3]

When I first read that, it hit me as an opportunity for God to bless his people with healing, health and joy. "Oh, the joys of those who are kind to the poor." You know, that's what Jesus did when he was on earth; he was kind to the poor.

Happiness and joy have often been far from me because of panic attacks. Yet, helping the poor opens the door for God to bless me with peace and joy.

I encourage you to find ways to help the poor. Whether it's an elderly home, a women's shelter, an orphanage or a downtown mission, take time to help those in need. Or support a church-affiliated relief department. Ask God to show you how you can reach out.

POINTS TO PONDER

1. When times get tough, do you usually think about yourself or others? In what ways would it help to get your mind off of yourself for a while?
2. Have you ever volunteered to help the poor in some way? If so, how did you feel afterwards?
3. List some practical ways that you can begin to help the poor in your community.

PRAYER

Father, you have promised that if I help the poor, you will, in turn, help me and heal me. Show me ways to be "kind to the poor," and allow me to find new happiness and peace in the process.

[1] Deuteronomy 28, paraphrased
[2] Romans 10:9, paraphrased
[3] Psalm 41:1,3 NLT

Notes: _____

_____
_____
_____
_____
_____
_____
_____
_____
_____

HONOR YOUR MOTHER AND FATHER

Honor your father and your mother, as the Lord your God has commanded you, that your days may be long, and that it may be well with you in the land which the Lord your God is giving you."[1]

Some of us have had wonderful, supportive parents. Others, abusive parents. Some parents have played an active role in our lives. Some, a passive role. For some of us, talking about parents brings up comforting childhood memories. For others, the memories are stained with pain and rejection.

This command from Deuteronomy is listed as one of the Ten Commandments.[2] Ephesians 6:2 tells us that this is the first commandment with a promise. What is that promise? "...that it may go well with you and that you may enjoy long life on the earth."[3]

If this promise is true, then the opposite is also true—that is, if we dishonor our mother and father, then it is possible that all may not go well and our life may be shortened.

But you don't know what my father has done. My mother abandoned me as a child, and I can't honor her. I had no real parents.

Bitterness towards anyone—especially parents—can destroy the soul.

My relationship with my father was a rocky one for years. As I completed high school, my rebellion reached a peak. College for me was: "See ya, Dad!" I was ready to explore the "real world." And did I ever!

Yet, the bitterness toward my father grew and grew, and I blamed him for my panic attacks. *If only he had loved me and raised me right...* I was so ungrateful. I took advantage of him and the things he did for me.

Soon, I came to realize that my dad did the best he could. He loved me in his own way. After my little boy was born, I quickly learned that being a father is no small task. I began to see all the things my father had done for me. To show him how much I appreciated this, I wrote him a letter apologizing for taking him for granted and for dishonoring him.

I overcame a lot of bitterness to settle things with my dad. It wasn't easy, but I know that God granted me the strength to make it through. And, God desires to help you as well. Let God be your new Father. Let him help you resolve situations with your earthly parents. He will show you how to honor them and respect them.

POINTS TO PONDER

1. Write down words that describe your parents or your relationship with them (ex. loving, explosive, strained, etc.) If most of these adjectives tend to be negative, ask God to show you how he sees them. What are some of their positive qualities?
2. Have you honored your parents the way God has commanded you to?
3. Ask God to show you any area of your life, in regard to your relationship with your parents, which needs healing. Is it possible for you to restore a relationship that's been broken? If not, then ask God to show you how you can make things right.

PRAYER

Father, if there is any area of my life in which I have dishonored my parents, I ask you to forgive me. If possible, show me how I can restore a right relationship with them. If not, then show me how to receive your grace so that I can find healing. Give me the strength to achieve this that all may go well with my family and me and that my days may be long.

[1] Deuteronomy 5:16, NKJV
[2] Exodus 20:12
[3] Ephesians 6:3, NIV

Notes:
_____
_____
_____
_____
_____
_____
_____

STICKS AND STONES

One of the world's top gymnasts, Christy Henrich dreamed of going to the Olympics. At a meet in Budapest in 1988, a judge told her that she was too fat and needed to lose weight if she wanted to make the Olympic squad.

Over a period of six years, Christy's health and life plummeted along with her weight. Anorexia set in. Her organs eventually failed due to malnutrition, and her life ended virtually before it began.

"Sticks and stones may break my bones, but words will never hurt me."

It is a taunt you probably know all too well. Perhaps kids teased you as a child, mocking your every step. Your defense, your retaliation, came in the form of this adage. It protected your ego while denying the truth:

Words *do* hurt.

Words *are* sometimes painful.

Words *can* break your spirit.

The words we speak carry power. Power to bless. Power to curse. Anxiety, fear and depression can be the result of negative words spoken over our lives.

"You will never achieve anything."

"You can never change."

"You will always be a failure."

Do words like these sound hauntingly familiar? Maybe a parent, a relative, a teacher, a sibling, a friend said something like this to you. Rather than challenge it, you agreed.

"The tongue has the power of life and death, and those who love it will eat its fruit."[1]

Since our words have the power of life and death, let us learn to speak the "truth in love"[2] and to "encourage one another daily...so that none of you may be hardened by sins' deceitfulness."[3]

142

POINTS TO PONDER

1. Ask God to reveal any negative words or curses that have been spoken over your life. Make a list of these.
2. Have you spoken similar words to others? If so, add these to your list. Did you witness the impact of these words?
3. Pray over each item on your list, asking God to heal you and the others who may have been affected by those words.

PRAYER

Father, help me to understand this truth regarding the power of our words. Show me if there have ever been any negative words spoken over me. Help me to receive your words of blessings and health as healing from those negative words. Also, help me to speak blessings rather than curses to others, that I may impart life and not death.

[1] Proverbs 18:21, NIV
[2] Ephesians 4:15, NIV
[3] Hebrews 3:13, NIV

Notes:

THE PRODIGAL

I heard a story one time about how shepherds dealt with wayward sheep. When a rebellious sheep would repeatedly drift off from the flock, the shepherd would be forced to break one of its legs. Then, he would gently bind it up and carry the sheep from pasture to pasture as he lead the flock. While the injured sheep could not walk, it depended completely on the shepherd. Later, after the leg was healed, the sheep still stayed close to the shepherd and never drifted away again.

"Blessed is the man whom God corrects; so do not despise the discipline of the Almighty. For he wounds, but he also binds up; he injures, but his hands also heal."[1]

Am I saying that panic attacks are discipline from the Lord? Maybe for some. For others, maybe not. I do know that these attacks force me to stay close to my Shepherd. When I drift away from him, things all around me seem to crumble, and the anxiety increases. My only choice is to run back to him.

Let me give you a more personal story:

My dad is a dog trainer. One particular dog he had was a great hunting dog, but he wouldn't obey. My dad would send him out for a bird, and the dog would sniff it out. But, after that, he would run off somewhere and not come back for quite a while. Since my dad hunted near highways and rivers, it was dangerous for the dog to stray off. So my dad bought a shock collar.

Soon, the dog took off again. He had run so far away that I could barely see him. Then, my dad pressed the button, and you could hear a faint "arrrf." In the distance, you could see the dog high-tailing it back to where we were. He wasn't walking—he was running. After two episodes with this collar, the dog never needed it again.

Do you think God takes pleasure in allowing these attacks to come? Do you think the shepherd enjoys breaking the leg of his sheep? Do you think my dad was excited about shocking the dog? No. Is this temporary pain needed? In some cases, yes.

In my life, I feel like panic attacks are God's shock collar for me. Spiritually, I drift away from my Shepherd. I hear my Master's voice at a distance, but I don't come running. I continue wandering

144

further and further away—sometimes into dangerous areas. Yet, one attack gets me high-tailing it back to God as fast as I can run.

POINTS TO PONDER

1. In what ways have you strayed from your Shepherd in the past?
2. Has God ever "broken your leg" in order to keep you close to him? Describe.
3. How does it make you feel to know that God may allow some pain in your life to bring you back to him?

PRAYER

Father, you are the Good Shepherd. Thank you for caring enough about me to "break my leg" when necessary and to carry me on your strong shoulders. Continue to do whatever it takes to keep me close to you.

[1] Job 5:17-18, NIV

Notes:

_____

_____
_____
_____
_____
_____
_____
_____
_____
_____

CONSEQUENCES

Caleb's inquisitive curiosity keeps him active. Exploring, learning, touching, experiencing. A child's mind is a sponge that absorbs everything it encounters. Yet, with this innate desire to explore, there exists the danger and pain of consequences.

We repeatedly told Caleb, "Do not touch the oven. It's hot. It could hurt you." Our commands were not to hinder his curiosity, but to protect him—to keep him from harm.

My wife had prepared some wonderful, homemade pizza for dinner one night. As I stood at the counter, I opened the door of the preheated oven. When I turned around to get the pizza, Caleb walked around behind me out of my sight and methodically placed both hands on the inside of the hot oven door. I turned back around just in time to see him scream. My heart broke.

After a quick visit to the emergency room, the doctor diagnosed Caleb with second-degree burns on the palms of both hands. Over the next few weeks, we kept ointment, bandages and socks on his hands. Thanks to God, there was no permanent damage.

When our Father sets boundaries in our life, it's because he loves us and does not want to see us hurt. He is not stifling our curiosity or creativity with his commands. He is protecting us from physical, mental and spiritual harm.

If we disobey our Father, there will be consequences. The aftermath of disobedience may be felt in different ways. For some, the results are immediately obvious and painful. For others, the pain is hidden and not so obvious. Regardless of how it is felt, there is no avoiding the consequences of disobedience.

"A man reaps what he sows."[1]

Just as my heart broke to see my son experience the consequence of disobedience, your Father hurts when you hurt. He does not like seeing you in pain. He comes to you ready to work with you on the pain. He's there to comfort and love you.

If you are hurting, talk to your Father. He knows all about it. You may not even know why you hurt. Ask God to speak to you through prayer and through his Word. Let the Holy Spirit speak through your conscience. Listen for his voice of compassion. Let the healing process begin.

146

POINTS TO PONDER

1. In what ways has your curiosity led you to go against what God told you not to do?
2. Have you been "burned"? Describe.
3. Have you allowed God to heal those burns with the salve of his Spirit, the bandages of his mercy?

PRAYER

Father, I know that your commands are for my good, to keep me from harm and pain. However, my humanity leads me to stray from your path into the dangerous land of the unknown. Forgive me for my stubborn independence, and heal the hurts I have brought upon myself.

[1] Galatians 6:7b, NIV

Notes:
_____
_____
_____
_____
_____
_____
_____
_____
_____
_____

THE OPPORTUNITY TO FAIL

Fear of failure has dominated my life for years. The need to succeed has driven the direction of my life. Always wanting to be good at what I do, I placed a high standard of accomplishment upon myself. Other times, people put those expectations on me.

But, fear of failure can have negative consequences. "Well, I can't really do that, because I might not be able to finish." Or does this sound familiar: "Even though I want to write a book, drive a car, get married someday, I just don't want to risk the chance of failure."

A few years ago, I was praying about these expectations that were driving my life. I prayed, "Lord, I hate feeling like I have to accomplish everything and do everything. It's just too much of a burden. I don't want to fail these people. I don't want to fail myself. And most of all, I don't want to fail you."

Then, I started thinking about my son. "Can he fail me?" No, he's my son. He's young and learning. He's curious, but transparently honest. Yes, he makes mistakes at times, but he has never failed me. I love him for who he is, not for what he does.

It was at that moment that I felt God say to me the same words, "Russell, you are spiritually young, and you are learning. You are curious, but honest. You make mistakes at times, but you have never failed me. I love you for who you are, not for what you do."

"For I am convinced that neither death nor life, neither angels nor demons, neither the present nor the future, nor any powers, neither height nor depth, nor anything else in all creation, will be able to separate us from the love of God." [1]

Immediately, I felt as if God had released me from all of the expectations he had on me—succeeding, achieving, accomplishing, always moving forward, never failing. I felt like he had given me the opportunity to fail. Now, let me clarify one thing—God was not giving me a license to disobey. God calls us to obedience. But, I felt he was giving me the opportunity to fail.

I encourage you to pray and ask God to show you what he requires of you. I think if you really listen and read the Bible, you will find that God loves you for who you are, not for what you accomplish. Jesus explains the only two requirements that are required of us: Love the Lord your God with all your heart and with all your soul and with all your mind, and love your neighbor as yourself.[2]

This week, find some way to invest your "talents", take some Godly risks and don't be afraid of failing. God loves you for who you are.

POINTS TO PONDER

1. What are some of your expectations? What expectations have been placed on you? List them.
2. Are these expectations from God, yourself or someone else?
3. Take your list of expectations and pray over them. Ask God to show you what expectations are from him and which ones are not.

PRAYER

Father, please reveal to me any unhealthy expectations. Show me your expectations. Show me how to release those things that are not of you. Open up my heart to receive your love.

[1] Romans 8:38-39, NIV
[2] Matthew 22:37-39, paraphrased

Notes:
_____
_____
_____
_____
_____
_____
_____
_____
_____
_____

YOUR FATHER'S INVITATION

One day, I was busy working on my computer when my son stumbled into the room with a handful of toys. He was ready to play, but I really didn't want to be disturbed at that time. I had so many things to take care of.

"Caleb? Would you please go into your room and play?"

Instead of responding to my request, he just plopped down and began to play. I was quick to respond. "Caleb!" I said with a stern voice. His eyes instantly shifted to mine. He knew from the tone of my voice that he had done something wrong.

When I looked into his eyes, my heart melted. Just by raising my voice slightly, I had pinched his tender heart. His eyes expressed the hurt, the condemnation. I quickly got up and started talking with Caleb. I wanted to make things right with him.

Afterwards, I wondered how God, my Father, would have handled a situation like that. How would he deal with outright rebellion to a command? Would he raise his voice? Would he knowingly hurt me with piercing words?

No. I don't think he would.

God is a caring Father, full of compassion and mercy, delicately approaching his children. His voice is tender and gentle—a voice of love—not harsh or condemning. I'm not saying that God does not punish his children, for he disciplines those he loves.[1] But when you fail, your Father woos you and draws you back to him. He doesn't bite back with devastating words. He wants you to come and sit in his lap and talk about what happened.

"Come now, let us reason together," says the LORD. "Though your sins are like scarlet, they shall be as white as snow; though they are red as crimson, they shall be like wool."[2]

Your Father invites you to talk with him about your mistakes and failures. Tell him your needs, your desires, your weaknesses. Share you heart, and he will share his.

POINTS TO PONDER

1. How do you respond to others when they interrupt your routine or disrupt your schedule?
2. What if God responded that way when you approach him with a need?
3. How long has it been since you have talked with God about your weaknesses, your needs, your dreams? Talk with him now.

PRAYER

Father, thank you that you gently correct me, that you invite me to come to you and share my heart. Help me to treat others with this same tender love.

[1] Proverbs 3:12a, paraphrased
[2] Isaiah 1:18, NIV

Notes:
_____
_____
_____
_____
_____
_____
_____
_____
_____
_____

YOUR CONSCIENCE

Have you ever felt that something you were doing was not right? Maybe it was gossiping about someone or not working the full eight hours your employer paid you for. Your conscience pierces your heart. Looming in the back of your mind, you hear, "I shouldn't do that." That is probably the voice of your Father nudging you on to righteousness.

Your conscience is one of the many ways God speaks to you. When the Holy Spirit whispers to you, your heart can hear his gentle, guiding voice. In fact, I believe it is the most common way he draws us and leads us to right standing with him and with others.

Luke knew about this subtle voice of the Almighty. He knew that the Holy Spirit commonly speaks through our conscience, **"So,"** he said, **"I strive always to keep my conscience clear before God and man."**[1]

With God, the quiet voice of your conscience will lead you and guide you into a wonderful fellowship with your Creator. It will reveal to you sin and areas of your life that need confession and repentance. The conviction of God is a blessed gift, for without it, we would continue down our path to destruction.

With man, your conscience will convict you when you have wronged someone. God requires that we forgive people as we have been forgiven. Do you still hold a grudge against someone? A grudge is nothing more than a hardened heart toward your conscience.

Do not harden your heart to the voice of God. Ask him to speak through your conscience as loud as he possibly can. When you listen to God through your conscience, you open a door to freedom that leads to peace.

Let your Father call to you, direct you and lead you to a place of rest. Let him speak through your conscience.

POINTS TO PONDER

1. Do you strive to keep a clear conscience before God and man?
2. Are you struggling with your conscience right now? If not, is it because you have already confessed your sin or because you have allowed your heart to become hardened to the voice of the Lord?
3. Describe how a clear conscience leads to peace?

PRAYER

Father, thank you that you speak to me through my conscience. Keep any callousness from my heart, so that I may be ever sensitive to your voice, opening the doorway to freedom and peace.

[1] Acts 24:16, NIV

Notes:

_____

_____

_____

_____

_____

_____

_____

_____

_____

_____

THE HARDNESS OF YOUR HEART

For this people's heart has become calloused; they hardly hear with their ears, and they have closed their eyes. Otherwise they might see with their eyes, hear with their ears, understand with their hearts and turn, and I would heal them."[1]

Our heart can be as tender as a rose bud or as hard as a cannonball. You are the one who determines how hard or soft your heart will be. When the Holy Spirit begins to "speak" to your conscience, how you respond determines the hardness of your heart.

Do you attempt to justify your actions against a person who has wronged you or wronged someone you love? "Well, you don't know what she did." Do you push the voice of God aside? "Well, she deserved it. She shouldn't have been nosing around in other people's business."

When you constantly ignore that whisper of conviction, you will come to a point where you can hear it no more. Your heart will become calloused in that area, and your future may be filled with bitterness and hatred.

Too many people harden their heart to the voice of God. Gentle guidance from the Spirit of God is stuffed away or pushed aside for the sake of our will. We have our agendas, our plans, our ambitions at stake. We dare not listen to God because he might tell us to do something we don't want to do. We question God's love for us.

Whether your heart is soft or surrounded by a brick wall, God will break through. The more tender your heart, the more easily God can get through to you. If your heart is hard, God may have to use some extreme measures to penetrate, but he will get through. Let him break down those barriers that have kept him out of your heart.

"I will give you a new heart and put a new spirit in you; I will remove from you your heart of stone and give you a heart of flesh."[2]

154

POINTS TO PONDER

1. Recall a time when the Holy Spirit convicted you. How did you respond?
2. Do you find yourself wrestling with your conscience? Do you continue to shut out that nagging voice until you can barely hear it anymore?
3. Is your heart tender before God, or are there some areas that may have been hardened over the years? Describe.

PRAYER

Father, speak to me through your Holy Spirit. Reveal any hardness of my heart and soften any calluses that may have formed. Finally, give me the strength to act upon my conscience, upon your leading.

[1] Acts 28:27, NIV
[2] Ezekiel 36:26, NIV

Notes:
_____
_____
_____
_____
_____
_____
_____
_____
_____
_____

THE CLOUDS OF SIN

I enjoy flying. Traveling at 30,000 feet provides such a breathtaking view of God's beautiful creation. On one particular flight, as the pilot started his slow decent, he announced that the weather in Dallas was overcast, muggy and cold. Yet, as we flew high above the clouds, the sky appeared clear and beautiful. The warmth of the sun beamed through the tiny window, and I could see for miles. The land below was covered with a thick layer of clouds resembling a fluffy blanket of pure, white cotton.

The plane tilted and began its dive into the thick, blinding stratum of white. As we entered the clouds, the brightness of the sun immediately turned dim. A thick haze quickly replaced my clear view of the heavens. I could barely see beyond the tip of the wing. For a few minutes, I lost all sense of direction in the confusion of the clouds.

As we slowly descended below the clouds, the murky weather became obvious. I could see the ground, but it was dark and dreary. I realized that this is what sin is like.

Walking with our Father with a pure conscience—blameless and cleansed—is a wonderful gift. We can feel the warmth of his presence and see clearly with eyes of understanding. There's no confusion, no darkness. All is beautiful in the light of God's grace.

When we sin, the light and warmth of God's presence grows dim. We enter into the clouds of confusion and chaos. We can no longer see clearly because the gloomy weather of our soul becomes overcast with guilt and shame. Fear soon follows.

As Ezra prayed, " . . . our sins are higher than our heads and our guilt has reached to the heavens."[1]

What do we do? How do we respond when flying through the clouds of fear and guilt?

"If we confess our sins, He is faithful and just to forgive us our sins and to cleanse us from all unrighteousness."[2]

Our Father is a forgiving Father. There is no God like him. Call upon his mercy. Call upon his strength to pull you up high above the clouds of sin.

156

POINTS TO PONDER

1. Has sin in your life sent you into the clouds of confusion and chaos? Describe.
2. Can you describe a time when you have confessed some sin and ascended from the depths of despair to the beautiful sky of a clear conscience?
3. Is there some sin you need to confess right now?

PRAYER

Father, forgive me of my sin. Thank you that when I confess my sins, you remove them as far as the east is from the west,[3] revealing a beautiful, Son-filled sky.

[1] Ezra 9:6b, NIV
[2] 1 John 1:9, NKJV
[3] Psalm 103:12, paraphrased

Notes: _____

_____

_____

_____

_____

_____

_____

_____

_____

_____

REFRESHING REPENTANCE

R epent, then, and turn to God, so that your sins may be wiped out, that times of refreshing may come from the Lord."[1]

The other day, I was playing racquetball with some friends. I hadn't played in months, so my endurance was not so enduring. We finished playing a match, and my mouth was parched. I desperately needed some water. I limped over to the water fountain and took a few drinks of the cold water. Ahh, it was so good! Each sip was so refreshing, so renewing. My strength returned, and I was ready for some more action.

God refreshes us in the same way. We are strengthened and renewed. We are alive again and ready for action.

How do we receive this refreshment from the Lord? How are we renewed and strengthened? In the above scripture, the first step is to "repent." Repentance leads to refreshment.

So, what is repentance? How do I repent? Is it simply a confession of the failures in my life? Is it acknowledging my sins before God and asking for forgiveness? It's all that and more. It's action. It's actively turning away from your sins and not going back.

When I was held in the grips of alcohol, I learned this principle first hand. After a binge, I would run to God and say, "Please forgive me. I repent. I'm sorry Lord." Yet, a few days later, I would give in and drink some more. The cycle of confession and concession would continue.

I confessed my sins, but I was waiting for God to somehow zap the desire to drink out of me. Then one day, I experienced a wonderful victory. I said, "Lord, from this day on, I choose not to drink anymore." I made the decision not to drink. That day, I experienced true repentance.

Repentance is a decision. It's confession. It's forgiveness. It's action.

When John was baptizing people in the Jordan River, he issued this challenge to the Pharisees and Sadducees: "Produce fruit in keeping with repentance."[2]

158

Do you hear what he was implying? It was as if he was saying, "Stop just mouthing the words of repentance, and act upon them! Let me see the fruit of your repentance."

I encourage you to ask your Father one simple question: "Lord, is there anything in my life of which I need to repent?" Listen carefully to your conscience. Then, act.

POINTS TO PONDER

1. Are you producing the fruit of repentance? Have you ever confessed your sin, only to go right back to your old ways? Describe.
2. Do you need some refreshment? Would you like a cool drink of God's forgiveness and mercy?
3. Ask, "Lord, is there anything in my life of which I need to repent?" Write down your convictions.

PRAYER

Father, reveal to me any sin of which I need to repent. Give me the strength to give up my worldly ways and turn to you so that I may receive a time of refreshing.

[1] Acts 3:19, NIV
[2] Matthew 3:8, NIV

Notes:
_____
_____
_____
_____
_____
_____
_____
_____
_____
_____

159

FORGIVING AND RELEASING

The man must have owed the king millions. The guards grabbed him one day while he was at work. They dragged him into the king's court. He didn't resist, for he knew why he was being summoned.

As he lay prostrate before the king, an attendant read a list of his debts. "Five and a half million dollars in taxes and penalties." The amount sent chills up the man's spine. He knew it was more than he could ever pay.

"Take this man, and throw him in jail," ordered the king. "We will sell his land, his children and his wife to pay off his debt. Then, he will work as my slave for the rest of his life."

The man began to weep. "Please be patient with me, king. I will pay back your debt. I love my family. Please do not take them away. I will do what it takes to pay you back."

The king was moved with compassion by the man's obvious cry for mercy. "Sir, I can see that your heart is broken. Today, let it be known that this man's debt is canceled. Nothing shall be required of him. Send him home to his family. Sir, you are a free man."

The man left for home free from his debts. As he crossed the street, he encountered one of his workers. In fact, this worker owed him 50 dollars. "Where's my money? You've owed me 50 bucks for almost a year. I want it now!"

The poor servant cried out, "Oh master, I know I owe you this money. Please give me some time to pay you back."

The man screamed, "No! I can't wait any longer. Off to jail until you pay it all."

One of the king's workers saw all this, and was amazed at how this man reacted. Word got back to the king, and the king summoned this man back to his court. "Sir, I canceled your debt of millions, and now you hold someone captive for 50 measly dollars? You will be punished." In anger the king turned him over to the jailers to be tortured, until he should pay back all he owed.[1]

Jesus told his followers, **"This is how my heavenly Father will treat each of you unless you forgive your brother from your heart."[2]**

160

It should be obvious from this parable that unforgiveness can lead to torment and torture. It may not be physical, but it is a torture of the soul that many of us know. Is there someone in your life you haven't forgiven?

If there is someone, ask God to show you how to release them. Forgiveness is a wonderful gift. We should share it with others.

POINTS TO PONDER

1. If I asked you to list all your debts, everything you've done wrong in your life, would it fill this page, this book, volumes?
2. Even after the huge debt of your sin has been canceled, do you still hold someone in bondage because of a wrong done to you?
3. Have you experienced torment because of this, or past unforgiveness? Describe.

PRAYER

Father, forgive my debts as I also forgive my debtors.[3]

[1] Matthew 18:23-34, paraphrased, [2]35, NIV
[3] Matthew 6:12, paraphrased

Notes:

_____
_____
_____
_____
_____
_____
_____
_____
_____
_____

WELCOME HOME

I love the parable of the prodigal son. It's a story about a young lad who was ready to strike out on his own, be his own man, break those parental ties and move on. It reminds me of myself when I went off to college. "Free at last! I can do what I want!"

Yet, in that dark season of my life, what I thought was freedom was nothing more than a numbing of the fear that plagued me. When I reached for a beer to numb the pain, I kept telling myself, "This is fun." But it wasn't.

I continued to deaden the fear—the fear of death, the fear of being out of control, the fear of loneliness. Yet, when the alcohol wore off, nothing had changed. My escape was not really an escape at all. My adventure into freedom was really a voyage into bondage.

As my life continued to spiral downward, I felt my heart being tugged another direction. I heard my Father's gentle voice calling me Home—a peaceful voice, not condemning, not demanding, not harsh, as I had expected. It was the voice of Love.

When I finally decided to go back Home, I was ready to work—to do whatever I could to make things right with God. After all, I had done so much wrong in my life, and I knew my Father would be mad.

As I drew closer to Home, I sensed that my Father was running to me. He was overjoyed to see me, to hold me, to talk with me. His love overwhelmed me. I didn't deserve such love; yet, he poured out such abundant grace and mercy. He held me and loved me just as I was.

"So he got up and went to his father. But while he was still a long way off, his father saw him and was filled with compassion for him; he ran to his son, threw his arms around him and kissed him."[1]

If you feel like you've drifted away from Home, call upon your Father in heaven. Humbly go back and confess your sin of independence. God will not turn you away. Rather, he will have compassion on you and love you—just as you are.

POINTS TO PONDER

1. In what ways have you, like the prodigal son, tried to find happiness and peace away from your Home?
2. Did these efforts work? Why or why not?
3. Have you returned Home to find your Father waiting for you? If not, would you like to?

PRAYER

Father, I thought that I could escape the fears on my own, yet I have ended up in the slop of a pig sty, just like the prodigal son. Thank you that you welcome me home with love, grace and mercy, and that you love me just as I am.

[1] Luke 15:20, NIV

Notes:
_____
_____
_____
_____
_____
_____
_____
_____
_____
_____

Smoldering Embers

ere is my servant, whom I uphold, my chosen one in whom I delight; I will put my Spirit on him and he will bring justice to the nations. He will not shout or cry out, or raise his voice in the streets. A bruised reed he will not break, and a smoldering wick he will not snuff out. In faithfulness he will bring forth justice; he will not falter or be discouraged till he establishes justice on earth. In his law the islands will put their hope."[1]

There are three aspects I find very encouraging in these prophetic verses about Jesus. First, he will not break or crush a bruised reed. What is this reed? A reed is like a branch, and, remember, we are the branches—he is the vine.[2] Jesus will not break us off; instead, he will handle us tenderly, allowing his life to flow into us to heal and restore our wounds.

Secondly, "a smoldering wick he will not snuff out." Do you sometimes feel like your life is simply smoldering? Only a few embers left. You were on fire when you were young—full of life and adventure. Now, your life seems on the verge of being snuffed out by panic and fear. Jesus did not come to snuff you out. He can take that glowing wick, and cause a new flame to burn in your heart, lighting the way for others.

Finally, "he will not falter or be discouraged till he establishes justice on earth." Do you know what that means? Jesus is not discouraged with you. You may feel like a failure, but Jesus will not falter or be discouraged with you. He is for you. He is on your side.

Today, be encouraged that Jesus' life is pulsing through your veins. The Holy Spirit is beginning to blow on those smoldering embers, ready to ignite a new fire in you—a fire not of fear and panic, but of joy and peace. A fire to love him more and to accomplish things beyond your imagination. He has high hopes for you. You can put your hope in him.

POINTS TO PONDER

1. Do you ever feel like a bruised reed? Why or why not?
2. Do you ever feel like a smoldering wick? Why or why not?
3. Do you ever feel discouraged by failure or slow progress? Describe.

PRAYER

Father, thank you that even before I began to delight in you, you delighted in me. Thank you that you will always handle me with care and will employ your Spirit to breathe new fire into my soul. Help me to place my hope in you, never becoming discouraged to the point of quitting.

[1] Isaiah 42: 1-4, NIV
[2] John 15:5, paraphrased

Notes:
_____
_____
_____
_____
_____
_____
_____
_____
_____
_____

THE WORK OF GOD

If you were asked to do the "work of God," what would you do?

Help the poor and needy?
Volunteer at an orphanage?
Donate money to suffering people?
Assist at the local mission?
What work is the work of God?

Even Jesus' followers asked, "What must we do to do the works God requires?"[1] I think this is a question we all ask ourselves: "What does God want me to do?"

Jesus answered, "The work of God is this: to believe in the one he has sent."[2]

The work of God is simply this: to believe in Jesus. This sounds strange at first. You'd think the work of God would involve laboring for a good cause or sacrificing your time and energy for someone else. No.

Believing in Jesus is all the work God requires of us. When we focus our energy on believing in Jesus, becoming like Jesus, loving Jesus, sharing Jesus, then we are doing the work of God. Activities like helping others, giving to the poor, praying for people or visiting the sick are all extensions of believing in Jesus. The more we love Jesus, the more we desire to love others.

When you believe in Jesus with all your heart, the work of God will come naturally. In fact, it won't be work at all. When our focus is Jesus, then the work of God is not work, but love expressing itself. It is God working through us.

Let me encourage each of you to do the work of God—to believe in Jesus. Learn more about Jesus, talk to Jesus, imitate the life of Jesus. In doing so, you will be doing the work God requires.

POINTS TO PONDER

1. Do you feel you must act a certain way in order to please God? List examples of rules you feel you must follow, good works you feel you should perform, sacrifices you feel you ought to make.
2. Do you believe that Jesus is the Son of God and that he died for your sins? Do you believe that this is all it takes to become a child of God?
3. How does it make you feel to discover that this is all God requires of you?

PRAYER

Father, you say that I have already done all that is required by believing in your Son, and yet I so long to please you. As I communicate with you and your Son daily, help me to become more like him.

[1] John 6:28, [2] 29, NIV

Notes:

_____

_____

_____

_____

_____

_____

_____

_____

_____

_____

TAX TIME TESTING

April 15 was fast approaching. With all the papers in order, the CPA just needed to organize the forms and file them.

"You know sir," the accountant said, "the extra income from your wife's babysitting was not claimed by anyone. You don't need to claim it. There is no record of this income, so there is no way to track it. It's only $330. Don't worry about."

"What does the IRS require?" asked the curious young man.

"Well, actually, they do require that all income be reported, but I wouldn't worry about it. If you were audited, they couldn't find out about it."

The young man rolled the idea around in his head for a few minutes, and then responded, "No, please claim it anyway. If the IRS requires it, then it should be claimed."

This true story illuminates a virtue that is so rare these days: integrity. Although the IRS would never have known about this "side money," God would have known. You see, "He will bring to light what is hidden in darkness and will expose the motives of men's hearts. At that time each will receive his praise from God."[1]

Whether dealing with finances, faith or family, we should walk upright, blameless before the Lord. He will reward us for such character.

"In my integrity you uphold me and set me in your presence forever."[2]

With integrity comes his presence, and with his presence there is peace.

If you've let your integrity wane, it's not too late. God longs to restore you.

168

POINTS TO PONDER

1. Would you have reported the money? Why or why not?
2. What does your answer to #1 say about your integrity?
3. Do you deal with guilt or worry because you have not been as honest or honorable as you would have liked? If so, ask God to forgive you now.

PRAYER

Father, I want to be a person of integrity, upright and blameless before you. Forgive me where I have failed in the past, and replace those failures with your righteousness, that I may receive praise from you and dwell in your presence forever.

[1] 1 Corinthians 4:5b, NIV
[2] Psalm 41:12, NIV

Notes: _____

_____

_____

_____

_____

_____

_____

_____

_____

_____

MEASURING STICK

The New Testament overflows with Jesus' invaluable teachings, but so often I am unproductive and ineffective in my understanding of these truths. Sometimes they just don't seem real to me. Putting them into practice seems virtually impossible. *What am I doing wrong?*

Are you frustrated with God because you know you should have peace, yet you struggle to find relief from your fears? Does your fight with fear seem futile?

"For this very reason, make every effort to add to your faith, goodness; and to goodness, knowledge; and to knowledge, self-control; and to self-control, perseverance; and to perseverance, godliness; and to godliness, brotherly kindness; and to brotherly kindness, love.

"For if you possess these qualities in increasing measure, they will keep you from being ineffective and unproductive in your knowledge of our Lord Jesus Christ."[1]

This scripture makes it quite clear: you will not meet your potential if you do not posses these godly qualities. Not only that, you should possess them with "increasing measure."

Growth is a requirement in your spiritual walk with God. As children, we often measured our growth on a chart or doorframe. Yet, we somehow overlook the importance of measuring our spiritual growth. This passage describes the characteristics of Jesus, our spiritual Measuring Stick. If we "make every effort" to grow in these areas, we will be productive and effective as we become more and more like Christ. If not, we will remain defeated by fear and doubt.

Today, I urge you to seek after goodness, knowledge, self-control, perseverance, brotherly kindness and love. Pursue these heavenly attributes. Your knowledge of Christ will grow. Your walk with God will be more effective.

POINTS TO PONDER

1. In what ways do you feel ineffective and unproductive in your spiritual walk?
2. Rate yourself on a scale from 0 to 10 (0 meaning that you possess none of that quality, 10 being perfect) on each of the characteristics mentioned in 2 Peter 1:5-7:
   - Faith
   - Goodness
   - Knowledge
   - Self-Control
   - Perseverance
   - Brotherly Kindness
   - Love

   Look back at this list over the next several months to see if you are growing.
3. List some specific ways you can strive to possess these qualities with "increasing measure."

PRAYER

Father, I often feel defeated as a Christian; yet, I desire to be more like your Son, Jesus Christ. Help me to grow in goodness, knowledge, self-control, perseverance, brotherly kindness and love, possessing these qualities with "increasing measure."

[1] 2 Peter 1:5-8, NIV

Notes:
_____
_____
_____
_____
_____
_____
_____
_____
_____

WATER-WALKING

It was dark that night on the Sea of Galilee. Jesus told his disciples to take the boat out. Then, Jesus came to them walking on the water. At first, they were frightened. But Jesus spoke to them and calmed their fears.

As soon as Peter saw that it was Jesus, he asked him, "Lord, if it's you, tell me to come to you on the water."[1] So Jesus called Peter to come to him. Peter's faith must have been soaring. He climbed out of the boat and started walking on the water toward Jesus.

Can you imagine what must have been going through his mind? "I'm walking on water! This is incredible! I can't wait to tell my friends about this. Who will believe me?" The joy and excitement of experiencing this miracle must have been overwhelming.

Then, something happened. His focused shifted. As he walked towards Jesus, something else caught his attention. The wind and waves churned around him. A storm was brewing. Peter started to worry. "Oh no. This is getting a little unstable. I don't think I can do this anymore." His water-walking faith quickly succumbed to water-walking fear.

"But when he saw the wind, he was afraid and, beginning to sink, cried out, 'Lord, save me!'"[2]

When those fearful thoughts came crashing in, Peter did something very important: he cried out to Jesus for help. Jesus reached down and pulled him up, and they walked back to the boat.

The next time you step out of your comfort zone, remember two things: don't take your eyes off Jesus. If you do, you will only see the wind and waves of unstable circumstances, and your faith will falter.

Secondly, if you do start to sink, simply cry out, "Lord Jesus, save me!" He will reach down from heaven, pick you up and walk with you back to the safety of your boat. He will not let you drown.

172

POINTS TO PONDER

1. Do you feel like you need "water-walking" faith to accomplish the simple tasks in life? Describe.
2. As soon as you step out of your place of safety, do you feel like the situation around you starts getting out of hand? Do you feel unstable, fearful of the waves and wind that pound against your faith?
3. Can you describe a time when you felt as if you were sinking and cried out to the Lord? Did he save you?

PRAYER

Father, help me to keep my eyes always on you, unshaken by the storms surrounding me. Thank you that when I do take my eyes off you and feel myself sinking, all I have to do is call on you and you will save me from my fears.

[1] Matthew 14:28, [2] 30, NIV

Notes:
_____
_____
_____
_____
_____
_____
_____
_____
_____
_____

FOOTSTEPS IN THE SNOW

A man and his son were playing in the snow one day. Pointing to a tree off in the distance, the father said, "Son, let's have a contest. We will both walk straight toward that tree. The contest is not to see who gets there first. Rather, the winner is the one who can have the straightest path in the snow."

The son agreed, and the father said, "Go." As each one moved closer and closer to the tree, the son carefully placed one foot in front of the other. He watched his feet closely to make sure each step was exactly in line. He didn't rush. He stepped. Analyzed. Stepped. Verified. Stepped. On and on.

When the boy finally reached the tree, his father was already there waiting for him. As the son glanced back at the two paths, he noticed that his path snaked through the snow. His father's path, on the other hand, looked straight as an arrow. Dumbfounded, the son questioned, "I don't understand. I took my time. I watched each and every step. Yet, my path was crooked. Why?"

The father responded, "Son, to keep your path straight, don't watch where you step. Keep your eye on the goal."

What a paradox: when we walk step by step, focusing on our feet, we often stumble. But when we take our eyes off our steps and fix them on the goal, we can walk a straight and narrow path. We must fix our eyes on Jesus, the author and perfecter of our faith.[1]

Paul said, **"But one thing I do: forgetting what is behind, and straining toward what is ahead, I press on toward the goal to win the prize for which God has called me heavenward in Christ Jesus."**[2]

POINTS TO PONDER

1. Do you feel that your path to peace has been meandering around in the blizzard of fear? Why or why not?
2. Do you spend a lot of time in one spot, analyzing and verifying every option before taking a step? Describe.
3. Where are your eyes? Are they on each little step you take or are they on the Goal?

PRAYER

Father, as I focus my eyes upon Jesus and follow him in all my ways, make my footsteps straight—a perfect path to peace.

[1] Hebrews 12:2, paraphrased
[2] Philippians 3:13b-14, NIV

Notes:

_____

_____
_____
_____
_____
_____
_____
_____
_____

DIRECT LINE TO GOD

Job once said, **"God is not a mortal like me, so I cannot argue with him or take him to trial. If only there were a mediator who could bring us together, but there is none. The mediator could make God stop beating me, and I would no longer live in terror of his punishment. Then I could speak to him without fear, but I cannot do that in my own strength."**[1]

Before the days of Jesus, people could not talk directly with God. Everything had to filter through the high priest. During Yom Kippur, the high priest spoke with God on behalf of the Jewish people. However, even the priest could only converse with God one day out of the year; and, he was the only one who could do it.

Yet, when Jesus came to earth, died and rose again, he became our new High Priest. Jesus is exactly what Job had wished for. Consider the following:

- Job wished to meet God in court and for someone to make peace between him and God. Jesus is our Mediator.[2]
- Job wished for someone to decide our case. Jesus intercedes on our behalf.[3]
- Job wished for someone to remove God's punishment. Jesus took our punishment upon himself.[4]
- Job wished to speak to God without being afraid. Today, we can speak directly with the Father in the name of Jesus.[5]

Everything Job wished for in these few verses is here for us today.

Why this elaborate plan of intercession and acceptance through Jesus? God is a holy God and cannot look upon sin. Yet, knowing that we are born sinners, God, in his infinite wisdom, came up with the perfect plan for us to speak with him and worship him directly.

Because of Jesus, we can approach God without fear. Do not take this privilege lightly because Jesus paid the price with his life.

176

POINTS TO PONDER

1. Does God's punishment or "terror" sometimes frighten you? What does Isaiah 53:4-5 say about this?
2. Are you ever afraid to ask God for what you really want, total healing, for example?
3. Do you ever take your direct line to God for granted? And how can you work to prevent this kind of apathy?

PRAYER

Father, I know that I am a sinner and unworthy to speak to you. Thank you that in your infinite love and wisdom you created a way for me to come to you in personal prayer. Help me to never take this privilege for granted. Deepen my understanding of my relationship with you through your son Jesus. And I pray that as I grow in understanding, my prayer life, quiet time and worship with you would become more intimate.

[1] Job 9:32-35, NCV
[2] 1 Timothy 2:5, paraphrased
[3] Romans 8:34, paraphrased
[4] Isaiah 53:4-5, paraphrased
[5] John 16:23-27, paraphrased

Notes: _____

_____
_____
_____
_____
_____
_____
_____
_____
_____

OUR SPIRITUAL LAWYER

About three years ago, I was selected for jury duty. I wasn't too excited about the idea, but I enjoyed watching, learning and being a part of the judicial system.

The relationship between the defendant and his lawyer particularly amazed me. The lawyer did all the talking, negotiating, persuading and decision making. The defendant just sat there while the lawyer did all the work.

That's what I see Jesus doing in heaven right now for each of us. He is seated at the right hand of God the Father interceding for us.

"If anyone does sin, we have one who speaks to the Father in our defense—Jesus Christ, the Righteous One."[1]

Jesus is your spiritual Lawyer seeking God on your behalf. Even when you are weary and worn down, Jesus continues on. He is striving, pressing forward, moving ahead for *you*. Not just all of mankind, but he is talking to God for _____. (Insert your name.)

Isn't it a nice feeling to know that the Judge will not render a verdict until Jesus has finished his defense for you? What a peaceful feeling to know that he is there in heaven at the Throne of Justice speaking for you. And even more incredible, we have already won the case. He paid the price for our wrongs. He has served our time. He has endured our punishment.

Today, I would encourage you to rest in the fact that Jesus is interceding for you. He is on your side!

178

POINTS TO PONDER

1. How does it make you feel to know that Jesus, our one and only Mediator[2], is interceding on your behalf?
2. If you could hear Jesus speaking to the Father for you, what do you think he is saying?
3. Make a list of the things you think Jesus is lobbying for you about. Make a list of some things you would like him to ask the Father for on your behalf.

PRAYER

Father, help me to remember that Jesus is there, seated at your right hand, speaking for me. Give me the peace and courage that comes from knowing that my Savior is interceding for me.

[1] 1 John 2:1b, NIV
[2] 1 Timothy 2:5, paraphrased

Notes: _____

_____
_____
_____
_____
_____
_____
_____
_____
_____

SWAPPING PLACES

Inevitably as children do, my son got sick. Caleb's battle with fever, coughing and sleepless nights had worn us down physically and mentally.

One afternoon as Caleb took his afternoon nap, my wife and I rested from our wearisome week. As we prayed for Caleb, my wife began to weep. "I just wish I could be sick in his place," she cried.

I, too, would have done anything to swap places with Caleb. I wished it were me lying in bed with a fever and cold chills instead of him. I wanted to bear his sickness. At that moment, I understood more of my Father's heart toward us.

In the following scripture, the prophet Isaiah prophesied about Jesus and how he would bear our pain: "Surely he took up our infirmities and carried our sorrows, yet we considered him stricken by God, smitten by him, and afflicted. But he was pierced for our transgressions, he was crushed for our iniquities; the punishment that brought us peace was upon him, and by his wounds we are healed."[1]

Just as in *The Prince and the Pauper* by Mark Twain, the Prince of the Universe wants to trade places with you, a lowly sinner. In fact, he became a man and endured punishment for your peace. He is ready to take your place, if you will simply accept your status as a child of the King. He wants to carry your pain, your affliction, your burdens, your torment. He invites you to give him your fears, your doubts, your worries.

I believe with all my heart that healing and freedom can come to those who give themselves totally to Jesus. When you give your heart to him completely, he will take your pain and replace it with his peace and confidence.

If I had the power to swap places with my son, I would have done it in a heartbeat because I love him so much. How much more does Jesus love you?

180

POINTS TO PONDER

1. Have you ever wanted to swap places with someone? Describe.
2. Have you allowed Christ to take on your pain or your panic? If so, how has this made a difference?
3. Do you feel like a child of God? Why or why not?

PRAYER

Father, I know that from the first moment I believed in your Son as my Lord and Savior, I became your child. And though I know that Christ died to take my infirmities and sorrows upon his shoulders, to nail them to the cross, I continue to cling to them because I have grown used to them. I yield these to you now. From this day on, help me to live like the child of God that I am.

[1] Isaiah 53:4-5, NIV

Notes:
_____
_____
_____
_____
_____
_____
_____
_____
_____
_____

FORSAKEN FOR OUR SAKE

My God, my God, why have you forsaken me?"[1]
If I could sum up my entire experience with fear and panic with one Bible verse, it would be this one. Forsaken. Abandoned. Rejected by God. I have felt all these.

When quoting this scripture, I could have easily referenced Matthew or Mark's account of Jesus' last words.[2] But, for some reason, it's easier to imagine David saying those words—not the Son of God. Not the Messiah. Not the sinless, perfect Lamb of God.

I find it hard to imagine Jesus on the cross crying out to his Father, "Why have you left me?" Why would God reject his own Son?

Is it possible that Jesus, the Son of God, experienced fear while nailed to the cross? I can imagine many theologians and scholars scoffing at the idea of such a claim. But, I don't think it is a sin to experience fear. The sin comes from how we respond to that fear.

"This High Priest of ours understands our weaknesses, for he faced all of the same temptations we do, yet he did not sin."[3]

How could Jesus understand our fear had he not experienced it himself?

Think about the garden on the morning of his execution? Alone in prayer, Jesus asked his Father *three* times if there were any other way. "My Father! If it is possible, let this cup of suffering be taken away from me"[4] Did he experience fear? Did he know the pain, the suffering, the agony he would face? He did.

The key is how he responded to that fear: "Yet I want your will, not mine."[5] He didn't run. He didn't flee. He didn't call a legion of angels to come to his rescue. He didn't surrender to the fear. He surrendered to his Father.

When you feel alone, abandoned by God, know that God will not forsake you.[6] When tempted to surrender to the fear, surrender to God instead. When you do, your Father's hand will reach down from heaven and fill you with the peace and courage to trust him.

182

POINTS TO PONDER

1. Have you ever felt forsaken or abandoned by God? If so, when? Describe how you felt (feel).
2. Do you believe that Jesus truly understands how you feel? Why or why not?
3. Read Hebrews 13:5b. Write it down in your own words.

PRAYER

Father, you have promised me that you will never leave me nor forsake me, yet sometimes I feel so alone, so afraid. You turned your back on your own Son because he took my sin upon himself so that you will never have to turn your back on me. Help me to surrender to you instead of fear.

[1] Psalm 22:1a, NIV
[2] Matthew 27:46, Mark 15:34
[3] Hebrews 4:15, NCV
[4] Matthew 26:39a, [5] 39b, NCV
[6] "Never will I leave you; never will I forsake you." Hebrews 13:5b, NIV

Notes: _____

_____
_____
_____
_____
_____
_____
_____
_____
_____

A Pure Joy?

Consider it pure joy, my brothers, whenever you face trials of many kinds, because you know that the testing of your faith develops perseverance. Perseverance must finish its work so that you may be mature and complete, not lacking anything."[1]

"Consider it pure joy..." What? A pure joy? How can I consider this fear, this panic, this pain a pure joy? The battle is too strenuous. The nightmare too real. It seems the fear does nothing but tear down and destroy. Destroy my peace, my sleep, my desires, my dreams.

And it's not just one trial, but "trials of many kinds." Oh Lord, help me! Why so many trials?

"...because you know that the testing of your faith develops perseverance. Perseverance must finish its work so that you may be mature and complete, not lacking anything."

If I wanted to teach my son how to swim, I could read to him the various techniques. I could teach him how to hold is breath. I could talk about the water, and how to stay afloat. We could even go down to the pool and watch people swim. But eventually, he would have to get into the water. In fact, the best situation would be to teach him while he was in the water. That's where he would learn the fastest.

Many of us are "in the water" of fear. You can read and study and learn all day long about what you should do, but eventually you will need to get "in the water." God builds our perseverance by daily testing our faith. That's the only way he can teach us to trust him.

POINTS TO PONDER

1. List some of the many trials you face? Do you consider these trials "pure joy"? Why or why not?
2. Do you know what it's like to press on day after day with the same old thoughts, same old fears? Did you realize you are developing perseverance?
3. What good things do you lack? Peace? Freedom from all fears? To be a good swimmer in the midst of trials?

PRAYER

Father, I admit that it is difficult for me to consider my trials a joy. However, I pray that this testing will strengthen me and build my faith so that I may be mature and complete, not lacking anything.

[1] James 1:2-4, NIV

Notes:

_____

_____

_____

_____

_____

_____

_____

_____

_____

_____

Death Brings Life

In January of 1992, I met a young lady named Angela at church. Over the next few months, our friendship grew. In fact, my feelings for her grew beyond friendship, and I began to desire a closer relationship. However, she didn't share those same feelings. It was as if she had recited those painful, grade-school words, "But, Russell, I just like you as a friend." *Ahhhhh!*

Finally, on the Fourth of July weekend, my emotions seemed to be caught up in a whirlwind—a tornado, to be exact—a jumble of love and rejection. That Sunday, I wrote her a letter explaining my feelings for her and her lack of feelings for me. I understood her situation, but I told her that I had to let this relationship die—friendship and all. If I couldn't have a close relationship, then I couldn't have a relationship at all. It was just too painful.

She read the letter and agreed. I remember driving home that night thinking, "Well, I did it. I wrote the letter. She knows it's over. It's done. It's over." But in my heart, I still had not let her go. I remember hearing that still, small voice say, "Now Russ, is it really over in your heart? Have you accepted that it is over?" At that point, I began to weep, grieving the loss of my friend.

Three days later, Angela called me. She had talked with her dad. She had talked with some friends. She realized that she did have feelings for me. (I knew it all along!) We married six months later.

Why this personal story about me and my wife? There is a principal here about God and how he works. At first, I poured so much into the relationship, yet it came up fruitless. I came to a place where I had to give the relationship to God—I had to let it die. I even grieved in my heart that it was over, as far as I was concerned. But on the third day, the relationship rose again. This time, with new life. This time, with new meaning.

"How foolish! What you sow does not come to life unless it dies."[1]

You can hold a seed carefully in your hand forever, but it will never come to life. You must bury the seed and let it die before it will bear fruit. This is a natural *and* spiritual principle.

POINTS TO PONDER

1. Is there any area of your life into which you feel you have poured your heart and soul with little or no return?
2. Do you need to give this aspect of your life to God? Do you need to let it die?
3. List some practical ways by which you can relinquish control in this area.

PRAYER

Father, at the Cross of your Son, you ultimately revealed the principal of sowing and reaping, the principal of dying in order to live. I choose to let this aspect of my life die, believing that you will resurrect it with new life, new meaning and new direction.

[1] 1 Corinthians 15:36, NIV

Notes:
_____
_____
_____
_____
_____
_____
_____
_____
_____

OPENING OUR EYES

E arly Sunday morning, the women who had followed Jesus during his ministry had brought a report that his body no longer lay in the tomb. Not only that, these women had seen angels and reported that Jesus was alive!

"How could it be?" Cleopas, who had also followed Jesus throughout his ministry, argued with his friend as they walked from Jerusalem to Emmaus. The thoughts must have raced through their minds. After all, they had envisioned the Messiah as a great ruler and king over all the earth. This Jesus had been just like any other man. Yet, he was different. He spoke with power and authority. People's lives were changed with just one look into his eyes. The blind could see. The lame could walk.

"What are you talking about?" asked a curious stranger who joined them as they traveled down the dusty road.

"Are you visiting Jerusalem that you've not heard about this Jesus of Nazareth?" they questioned him.

Beginning with Moses and the prophets, the stranger opened to them the scriptures. He must have shared story after story about the suffering Messiah and God's plan for man. The two-hour journey must have been the most wonderful Bible study a person could have ever had.

Yet, as this man brought to life the Word of God, these two men could not even see that the Word of God incarnate stood before them. Their natural eyes were open, but their spiritual eyes were closed.

They completed their journey, and Jesus joined them for dinner. As he broke the bread, the men's eyes were opened and they recognized him. Immediately, he disappeared.

"Did not our heart burn within us while He talked with us on the road, and while He opened the Scriptures to us?"[1]

I find it so amazing that Jesus, the living Word of God, taught these men himself, but they could not recognize him. Yet, when the time was right, they could see.

Let Jesus open your eyes to see beyond what your natural eyes can see. Let him open up the scriptures to you.

POINTS TO PONDER

1. Do you feel that your spiritual eyes are sometimes closed, not seeing the work of the Lord in your life?
2. Does your heart burn to know him more?
3. Would you like Someone to open the scriptures to you—to explain passages you don't understand?

PRAYER

Father, open my spiritual eyes. Allow me to see your hands at work in the world around me. Permit me to feel your presence as I worship you at church and at home. Reveal to me truths from the scriptures that I may have overlooked or misunderstood in the past, that my anxiety may be put to rest.

[1] Luke 24:32b, NKJV

Notes:
_____
_____
_____
_____
_____
_____
_____
_____
_____
_____

OUR TUTOR

In high school, one of my favorite subjects was math. The formulas, expressions and rules came naturally to me. I enjoyed the challenge of working through and solving problems.

In college, I was able to use my math ability to tutor people who struggled in this area. I would walk them through the problems and explain the rules and procedures. I would remind them of what the teacher said and how to apply those teachings.

In our everyday life, we also have a Tutor—one who walks with us everyday, teaching and counseling. One who reminds us of what Jesus taught.

Jesus said, **"All this I have spoken while still with you. But the Counselor, the Holy Spirit, whom the Father will send in my name, will teach you all things and will remind you of everything I have said to you."**[1]

At this very moment, Jesus is seated at the right hand of the Father.[2] But, we are not left alone. Jesus sent us the Holy Spirit to be our link between heaven and earth, our line of communication between the natural and supernatural. The Holy Spirit comforts us and counsels us. He teaches us and reminds us of Jesus' teachings.

Do you have a hard time understanding the Bible? Ask the Holy Spirit to teach you as you read. Do you not know how to handle a certain situation? Ask the Holy Spirit to remind you what Jesus would do.

"Can I really hear the Holy Spirit?" you may ask. The answer is yes. The voice of our Father speaks through his Holy Spirit—like our long distance telephone link. As we talk and communicate with people over a telephone line, so we also can talk with our Father in heaven through his Holy Spirit.

Have you ever thought, "I really need to pray today"? That's the Holy Spirit reminding you. Have you done something you know was wrong? That "knowing" is the Holy Spirit convicting you.

The next time fear begins to rise up within you, listen carefully to the Holy Spirit. You will hear your Father say, "No need to worry. I will be with you. I will protect you. Trust me."

POINTS TO PONDER

1. Do you feel like you need a Tutor for life?
2. Have you ever heard the voice of the Holy Spirit speaking to your conscience? Describe a specific instance.
3. Write down some concepts from the Bible you don't understand, questions you would like the Holy Spirit to answer for you.

PRAYER

Father, thank you that I am not alone in my struggle against anxiety. Make my heart sensitive to your Holy Spirit as he speaks to my soul, revealing your truths, conveying your comfort.

[1] John 14:25-26, NIV
[2] Mark 16:19, paraphrased

Notes: _____

_____

_____

_____

_____

_____

_____

_____

_____

_____

191

THE LIVING WORD

I t's early Sunday morning as I write this, and it's still dark outside. I can hear the rain pounding on our roof. Lightening strikes off in the distance. The flash illuminates the room for a brief second. I wait. I listen. The booming thunder soon follows. As the rain trickles off the roof, I am reminded of a scripture about God's faithfulness:

"The rain and snow come down from the heavens and stay on the ground to water the earth. They cause the grain to grow, producing seed for the farmer and bread for the hungry. It is the same with my word. I send it out, and it always produces fruit. It will accomplish all I want it to, and it will prosper everywhere I send it."[1]

God's Word is so precious. It is our primary link between the natural and supernatural. As the Holy Spirit illuminates the Word of God to us, our spirit grows and our faith is strengthened. As surely as the rain comes, so God faithfully fulfills his Word.

The Word of God is not only a book of life; it is a living book. Hebrews 4:12a (NKJV) declares: "For the word of God is living and powerful..." It is living. It is powerful. You are not only reading history—you are reading Life!

Let me encourage you this week to sit down, take a break and read a few verses from the Bible. As you read, ask the Holy Spirit to show you some of God's promises. Ask him to show you new and exciting truths. Ask him to reveal your path to peace. Let him introduce you to the living Word of God, Jesus Christ.

POINTS TO PONDER

1. How often do you read your Bible? Do you feel you should read it more? Does it seem "alive" to you?
2. What promises has God revealed to you this week through his Word.
3. Does God seem faithful to you? Why or why not? Write down any past situations in your life where God proved himself faithful?

PRAYER

Father, reveal to me your faithfulness through your Word and through your work in my life. Make real to me your promises to help me through fear and anxiety, and allow me to find peace in those promises. Teach me to trust you with everything in my life.

[1] Isaiah 55: 10-11, NLT

Notes:
_____
_____
_____
_____
_____
_____
_____
_____
_____
_____

DESIRES OF THE HEART

Delight yourself in the Lord, and he will give you the desires of your heart."[1]

What are the desires of your heart?

To drive again.

To fly in a plane.

To go to college.

To spend time with loved ones.

To sleep peacefully.

To be free from all fear.

How can you attain these things? What effort and strength do you have to put into those desires to receive them? The scripture simply says to "delight in the Lord." When you delight in God, he will fulfill those desires. It's not something a person can do. God is the one who fulfills the desires of your heart.

"So, how do I delight in the Lord?" you may ask.

The Hebrew word for delight is *anag*, which means "to be soft, to be delicate, to be dainty. The connotation has to do with taste—to delight in a delicacy. You can almost taste it. Psalm 34:8 declares, "Taste and see that the LORD is good; blessed is the man who takes refuge in him."

To delight in the Lord, we must . . .

. . . rejoice in his faithfulness.

. . . worship him for who he is.

. . . praise him for his mighty deeds.

. . . take delight in his promises and his Word.

Make it a habit to delight in the Lord. Taste and enjoy his goodness. Soon, the desire of *his* heart will become the desire of *your* heart.

POINTS TO PONDER

1. Make a list of the desires of your heart. What do you want to accomplish in your life? What are your dreams, your hopes?
2. In what ways have you tried to achieve these desires in your own strength? Has it worked?
3. What does it mean to you to "delight in the Lord"?

PRAYER

Father, I long to delight in you. You say that you will bless me if I merely rest and enjoy you; and yet I'm not sure I know how to do that. Please help me to taste and see that you are good.

[1] Psalm 37:4, NIV

Notes:
_____
_____
_____
_____
_____
_____
_____
_____
_____
_____

EXPERIENCING WORSHIP

Oh come, let us worship and bow down; let us kneel before the LORD our Maker."[1]
I believe worship is our first priority here on earth. In Matthew 22:36-38 (NIV) a Pharisee asked Jesus, "Teacher, which is the greatest commandment in the Law?"

Jesus replied, "Love the Lord your God with all your heart and with all your soul and with all your mind. This is the first and greatest commandment."

If that's not worship, I don't know what is! Worship plays an integral part in our walk with God, and we should spend time each day in adoration of our Father in heaven.

God desires that we worship him "in spirit and in truth."[2] True worship exceeds any hollow act of homage for it overflows from our innermost being—our heart, our soul, our mind. Through worship we can enter into the Lord's presence, lavishing our affections on him and expressing a heart of gratitude and thankfulness toward the Giver of life.

There are times when I am worshipping God that I feel so much peace in who I am. All of my fears turn to tears of joy when I worship my Deliverer, my Shield, my Strength, my Father.

God pours out his wisdom when we worship him. God pours out his peace when we worship him. God pours out *himself* when we worship him.

When we worship God, we are filled with his attributes, his character. We experience his wisdom and peace. We experience God.

"How can I worship God?" you may ask.

You can sing to him. You can shout to him.

You can dance for him. You can pray to him.

You can lift your hands to him. You can bow before him.

You can praise him. You can honor him.

You can love him.

Experience God today. One moment in his presence can transform your life forever.

POINTS TO PONDER

1. When was the last time you really spent worshipping God?
2. Did you experience his presence, his peace during that time of worship?
3. Make a list of some ways you can worship your Father. Make it a goal to worship God in some form or fashion at least once a day.

PRAYER

Father, I desire to worship you more. Forgive me for not obeying the greatest commandment of all—to worship you with all my heart, all my soul and all my mind. Allow me to experience your transforming presence that comes from worshipping you.

[1] Psalm 95:6, NKJV
[2] John 4:24, NIV

Notes:

_____

_____

_____

_____

_____

_____

_____

_____

_____

FACT OR FEELING?

Do you ever feel forsaken by God? Abandoned? Rejected? Does God seem so far away that no matter how high you reach, he is unreachable still? Do you feel as if you are standing in a desert with no water, no shade, no rest in sight? Do you cry out in prayer but hear no obvious response to your pleas of desperation?

Job felt this way: "Why do you hide your face and consider me your enemy? Will you torment a windblown leaf? Will you chase after dry chaff?"[1]

King David experienced this loneliness: "Why, O LORD, do you stand far off? Why do you hide yourself in times of trouble?"[2]

The Bible is full of people who felt rejected and abandoned by God. Loneliness and rejection filled their hearts. Questions and doubts filled their minds when God didn't respond the way they thought he should.

Many times, what we feel and what is real are quite different. Our faith should not be based on our feelings, but on the truth. When you read through the Bible, you are reading truth. Applying that truth—even when your feelings are saying the opposite—is a bold step of faith.

God says: **"Don't be afraid.[3] I love you.[4] Trust me."[5]**

Throughout the Bible, we are instructed to trust God. Trusting God means that you don't follow your feelings—you follow God. Feelings can deceive you. Never trust your feelings when they go against the Word of God. The enemy will speak lies to your mind and cause your feelings to flounder. When you follow your feelings and let doubt rule in your mind, you will be "like a wave of the sea, blown and tossed by the wind."[6]

This is so true with fear and panic. Adrenaline races through your body. A tornado of feelings and doubts whirls through your mind. Yet, God says, "Don't listen to those thoughts. Trust me."

When you take that step of faith and trust God in the middle of your storm, God's hand will reach down and touch you. The peace and confidence of knowing God is there will flood your soul. It is a wonderful peace—a peace that passes understanding.

Today, open your heart to faith: faith to not follow your feelings; faith to listen to God; faith to trust your Father.

SEASON OF PEACE

POINTS TO PONDER

1. Describe how you *feel* right now?
2. Do these feelings coincide with the Word of God? Explain.
3. Write down several truths from the Bible that will help to combat any feelings of negativity or fear.

PRAYER

Father, I understand that your peace is not a feeling, but a fact. Remind me whenever I feel anxious or afraid that you will never leave me. Do not allow me to be fooled by fleshly feelings, but help me to live by faith in your unfailing truth.

[1] Job 13:24-25, NIV
[2] Psalm 10:1, NIV
[3] Luke 12:7, paraphrased
[4] Isaiah 43:4, paraphrased
[5] John 14:1, paraphrased
[6] James 1:6b, NIV

Notes:
_____
_____
_____
_____
_____
_____
_____
_____
_____
_____

199

THE DEPTH OF GOD'S LOVE

We cannot even begin to understand how much our Father loves us. If we could comprehend or fathom his love, it would overwhelm us.

For those of you with children, think about how much you love them. Or take someone who means the most to you—a spouse, a relative, a dear friend. You love them. But God's love transcends all those. We can never love someone or something more than God loves us.

In the third verse of the classic hymn, *The Love of God*[1], F.M. Lehman writes:

Could we with ink the ocean fill,
And were the skies of parchment made,
Were every stalk on earth a quill,
And every man a scribe by trade.
To write the love of God above,
Would drain the ocean dry,
Nor could the scroll contain the whole
Though stretched from sky to sky.

Interestingly enough, some of these words were found written on the wall of an insane asylum in the early 1900s and then arranged into this hymn.

What does this say about God's love? It says that God's love reaches even the deepest, darkest corners of the earth. As David said to God, " . . . if I make my bed in the depths, you are there."[2]

"And I am convinced that nothing can ever separate us from his love. Death can't, and life can't. The angels can't, and the demons can't. Our fears for today, our worries about tomorrow, and even the powers of hell can't keep God's love away. Whether we are high above the sky or in the deepest ocean, nothing in all creation will ever be able to separate us from the love of God that is revealed in Christ Jesus our Lord."[3]

How marvelous is the love of God!

200

POINTS TO PONDER

1. Who do you love most in this world? Describe your feelings toward him/her/them.
2. Have you ever felt that you are in a pit so deep God's love could never reach you? Explain.
3. Can anxiety, panic or fear separate you from the love of God?

PRAYER

Father, thank you that nothing can separate me from your wonderful love. Let the light of that love beam through my spirit today to cleanse and comfort my heart.

[1] Lehman, F.M. *The Love of God.* Arranged by Claudia Lehman Mays. Nazarene Publishing House, Kansas City, MO. 1945.
[2] Psalm 139:8b, NIV
[3] *Romans 8:38-39, NLT*

Notes:
_____
_____
_____
_____
_____
_____
_____
_____
_____
_____

MY PRIVATE JOY

I remember going to doctors as a child crippled by episodes of fear. "So tell me what you are experiencing," they would urge. I wouldn't know where to begin. How can you explain the unexplainable? How can you dig up those memories you've spent so much time and energy trying to bury?

After I was married, the attacks were still as intense. My wife would try to console me by saying, "It's okay, honey, I understand."

Talk about the wrong thing to say! I would get so mad: *You do not understand! You do not know what this is like!* How could she? She had never experienced a panic attack, and God forbid she ever would.

Anyone who has experienced the terror of anxiety and panic attacks knows the pain and discouragement that accompanies this paralyzing disorder. Yet, if you try to explain it to someone who has never experienced this type of fear, it is impossible for that person to understand.

"Each heart knows its own bitterness, and no one else can share its joy."[1]

Although no one on earth can share our individual pain, God offers us hope that we will experience a joy that is so special, so unique, so indescribable that no one else can ever understand it. What a wonderful promise!

Your joy may come through driving alone for the first time in years. Maybe it's flying on an airplane or going outside of your home. Maybe it's going to the grocery store. Maybe, it's just waking up in the morning excited about what the day has to offer.

When you talk with people who have made it through this "valley of darkness," they will tell you that the sunrise on the other side is more beautiful than they could have ever imagined.

POINTS TO PONDER

1. Recall a time when you explained a fearful episode to someone only to be stared at or misunderstood.
2. What are some typical responses you get from people when you tell them about your condition?
3. Write down some joyful times that you feel you may have never experienced were it not for your struggle with anxiety.

PRAYER

Father, I know the bitterness of fear—a pain that only you and I know. Your Word says that a special joy awaits me. Help me to see beyond the discouragement and fear—to the supernatural joy that comes from knowing you.

[1] Proverbs 14:10, NIV

Notes: _____

_____

_____

_____

_____

_____

_____

_____

_____

_____

LIVING IN THE PRESENT

Is time travel really possible? Physically, no. But traveling back and forth through time *mentally* is a common experience for many of us.

The past haunts many. For some, the past holds memories of wounds that have yet to heal. For others, it may be full of guilt and shame. The past can be a closet full of uninvited thoughts. When you open the door to that closet, you focus your attention on the "should have's" and "could have's."

The future can be a fearful place to live, as well. The bombardment of "what if's" wreaks havoc in your mind when you live for tomorrow. No one knows what will happen tomorrow or the next day, or the next. The future is a dark tunnel, never allowing you to see what lies ahead.

We can only truly live in the present. There is no way to physically escape it. No matter where you are or what time it is, it is always "now." The only time, the only breath, the only heartbeat you are guaranteed is the one you have right this instant.

God calls us to live in the present—physically *and* mentally. He does not want our minds drifting off into our forgiven past or wandering away into our unknown future. He wants us to focus on today. He wants us to listen to his voice today.

"Therefore do not worry about tomorrow, for tomorrow will worry about itself. Each day has trouble enough of its own."[1]

POINTS TO PONDER

1. Do you spend a significant amount of your mental energy in the past, the "should have's"? Describe.
2. What about the "what if's"? Do you worry about the future? Why or why not?
3. List some practical ways you can strive to remain in the present.

PRAYER

Father, cleanse me from the sins and heal me from the wounds of my past. Rescue me from the worries of the future, that I may take one day at a time, saying, "This is the day the Lord has made, let us rejoice and be glad in it."[2]

[1] Matthew 6:34, NIV
[2] Psalm 118:24, NIV

Notes:

_____

_____

_____

_____

_____

_____

_____

_____

_____

_____

DUE SEASON

I love autumn. As the hot, humid summers in Texas come to a close, the cool, brisk winds of fall are a welcome change.

As a kid, I longed for that cool breeze to blow in. It has always been my favorite time of year. A time of new clothes, new colors and new coolness. A time of electric blankets and electric heaters. A time of climbing trees and raking leaves. A time of harvest. It reminds me that one season is coming to a close, while a new season is about to begin—a season full of changes.

With panic attacks and crippling anxiety, we may feel like the same old season lingers on and on, never changing. The coolness of peace doesn't seem to blow into our lives. The leaves are always the same color. The monotony of life continues blandly day by day.

But God promises us change—a good change. We must diligently press on and seek God with all of our heart. We must continue to worship him and praise him, even when our life seems to be crumbling around us. When we do, a new season will blow into our lives.

"And let us not grow weary while doing good, for in due season we shall reap if we do not lose heart."[1]

Let me encourage you to press on, for your season of peace draws near. Can you feel the gentle breeze whispering to you? If not, call upon God to show you the new season that is coming upon you.

POINTS TO PONDER

1. Does your life seem monotonous or stagnant?
2. Are you ready for a spiritual change of seasons? Describe your "season of peace."
3. What would you like to reap in "due season"?

PRAYER

Father, the constant heat of anxiety has left me scorched. I long for the cool breeze of your Spirit to bring a change of season into my life. Reveal to me the peace that awaits me, as I promise to press on toward your perfect will.

[1] Galatians 6:9, NKJV

Notes:
_____
_____
_____
_____
_____
_____
_____
_____
_____
_____

NOTES

NOTES

NOTES

Made in the USA
Lexington, KY
22 July 2013